The Grand Adventure

A Year by Year History of Virginia

The Grand Adventure
A Year by Year History of Virginia

by

James A. Crutchfield

The Dietz Press

Copyright © 2005

ISBN: 0-87517-125-7
Library of Congress Catalog Number: 2004109852

ALL RIGHTS RESERVED
Printed in the United States of America

Published by The Dietz Press
Richmond, Virginia
www.dietzpress.com

Cover Design by Bob Oller

To Virginians Everywhere:
Past
Present
and
Future

Introduction

Do we need another history of Virginia? The answer is an emphatic yes, especially if it is THE GRAND ADVENTURE, "A Year by Year History of Virginia" by James A. Crutchfield.

Least we be accused of that well-known canard that we Virginians are unable to restrain our pride in our heritage, let us make it clear at the outset that the author is a Tennessean. This should provide Mr. Crutchfield with some objectivity, yet he writes about us with compassion, clarity and affection. In less expert hands the book could have become a straightforward chronology. But Mr. Crutchfield is no maker of lists. He has recognized the drama in our history and evokes it throughout. Even though we know the outcome we read with suspense about critical events in our past whether it is the struggle at Jamestown to survive or the damage we suffered in the winds of Hurricane Isabel.

The book is richly illustrated with etchings, maps and reproductions of paintings. Numerous anecdotes enliven the story:

"The first recorded theatrical presentation in the New World was given at Fowkes' Tavern in Accomack County. Entitled "The Bear and The Cub" the performance brought charges against its three producers "for acting a play!"

Depth and verisimilitude enhance familiar stories:

"General George Washington took his army into winter camp at Valley Forge, Pennsylvania. Before the next spring brought relief, three thousand American soldiers – 'without clothes to cover their nakedness, without blankets to lie on, without shoes for want of which their marches might be traced by blood from their feet' – had died from lack of food, medical supplies, and warm clothing."

If you thought you knew everything there was to know about Virginia you might be surprised. Did you know, for instance, the origin of the word "hundred" to describe an early plantation? Did you know what caused an early experiment with the "silk worm" industry to fail? Or what dignitary was entertained in the Williamsburg home of Mrs. Mary Monroe Peachy in 1824?

Every Virginian should read THE GREAT ADVENTURE. We have come upon a treacherous time and we live in an uncertain world. Now is a good time to look back on the Virginia story and to take courage and comfort from it and to carry it with us into the future.

We owe Mr. Crutchfield our gratitude. Since he had the misfortune to have been born outside our borders we should declare him an Honorary Virginian.

Earl Hamner

Table of Contents

The Grand Adventure
A Year by Year History of Virginia

Before Jamestown

The establishment of North America's first permanent English-speaking settlement at Jamestown in 1607 was preceded by a great deal of exploratory activity, not only by the English themselves, but by adventurers from other European nations as well. As soon as Christopher Columbus stumbled upon the New World in 1492, the Crowns of England, Spain, Portugal, Holland, and France quickly jumped into the arena and sent ships far across the Atlantic to exploit the newfound lands and to garner what treasures they could. The Jamestown adventure was simply the culmination of more than a century of continuous effort on the parts of many nations to establish influence and gain control of parts of the mysterious and unknown continent.

During the 1500s, much of New World was frequented by ships flying many different flags. The Spanish, undoubtedly the world's strongest seafaring nation at the time, explored and, in many cases, established strongholds in the West Indies, Mexico, and the present-day southeastern United States. In fact, in 1561, Pedro Meléndez de Avilés accidentally came upon the Chesapeake Bay, spent a few days in the area, and took Opechancanough, an older brother of the more famous Powhatan, back to Spain with him. Nine years later, when Opechancanough was returned to his own people, the Spanish churchmen who accompanied him established a short-lived Jesuit mission on the south bank of the York River.

By 1565, in the name of Spain's monarch, Philip II, De Avilés had established St. Augustine in Florida, the oldest surviving European-settled town in the United States. In the meantime, Frenchmen were making inroads into today's Canada, while their English counterparts concentrated on the mythical land that soon became known as Virginia.

Feisty Queen Elizabeth sat on England's throne at the time, and, in 1584, she issued to one of her court favorites, Walter Raleigh, a royal grant that gave him possession of a large tract of land in America. Raleigh wasted no time in sending out a party under the command of Philip Amadas and Arthur Barlowe to explore his new possessions. Landing in the neighborhood of today's Outer Banks of North Carolina, the Englishmen reported favorably to Raleigh upon their return home. Hoping to impress his virgin queen, Elizabeth, Raleigh named the recently visited territory "Virginia."

During the summer of 1585, Raleigh dispatched a colonizing party of some 107 prospective settlers to Virginia under the guidance of Governor Ralph Lane. The ships disembarked on Roanoke Island and over the next few months the entire region along present-day North Carolina's Atlantic coast was explored. The winter proved difficult, however, and, during the following summer when Francis Drake's small fleet called on the colonists,

Walter Raleigh's colonization project of 1587 proved to be disastrous and, when Governor John White returned to Roanoke Island three years later, his party found the settlement deserted. The mysterious word, "Croatoan," was carved on a giant tree, but otherwise, there was no clue as to the fate of the one hundred settlers.

From an old engraving in the author's collection.

the disheartened survivors jumped at the opportunity to leave the miserable place for England.

Two years later, Raleigh tried again to colonize his holdings. The new governor, John White, and about one hundred settlers returned to the area. After White assured himself that all was well, he set off for England to re-supply. By the time White actually revisited Roanoke Island – the departure from his homeland was delayed for three years due to England's and Spain's flirtation with war and the invasion threat by the Spanish Armada – all of his colony had perished, including his own granddaughter, Virginia Dare.

As the first decade of the seventeenth century progressed, the English renewed their efforts to occupy North America. By now, Elizabeth was dead, and the colonization failures of the late 1500s were history. Elizabeth's successor, thirty-seven-year-old James I, nursed grandiose plans for England's New World holdings, and in April 1606 he granted a charter to a group of English investors and businessmen for the formation of the Virginia Company. The Company was organized into two divisions – the Virginia Company of Plymouth with authority to colonize and administer present-day New England and the Virginia Company of London, whose oversight focused on the southern regions including Walter Raleigh's original Virginia colony. When a Plymouth colony soon failed, all eyes turned toward Virginia as the Crown's premier settlement experiment in America.

England's renewed Virginia adventure began in late December, 1606, when three galleons – the *Susan Constant, Discovery,* and *Godspeed* – slipped their moorings and drifted down the Thames River from London, soon to be engulfed by the mighty Atlantic Ocean. The ships were commanded by Captain Christopher Newport, a veteran seaman with the experience of several West Indian explorations under his belt. In late April, 1607, after an eighteen-week-long voyage, the small fleet sighted Cape Henry at the mouth of Chesapeake Bay.

For the next two weeks, Newport and his crew explored the numerous inlets, rivers, and marshes along the coast. Proceeding for about thirty miles upstream on one of the waterways, later named the James River in honor of the king, the three ships and the one hundred or so men and boys aboard sighted a spit of land that appeared particularly attractive for settlement. Newport gave the orders and the vessels moored in the brackish water surrounding today's Jamestown Island. The date was May 13, 1607, and it marks the birth of Virginia. The events that were about to unfold – and those that followed over the next four hundred years – are among the most interesting in American history. Here, then, Virginia's story, told year by year in chronological order.

1607

During mid-May, 1607, a group of 104 men and boys disembarked from their three ships alongside the Virginia shore and founded Jamestown, the first permanent English settlement in America. Unfortunately, the site they selected was ill-suited for European habitation due to the intense humidity, hoards of biting insects, and poorly drained cropland. The settlement experiment was also hampered by the fact that a large percentage of the group consisted of so-called "gentlemen," who had little or no practical skills that could contribute to the colony's success. Nevertheless, following an Indian attack, the adventurers built a small, triangular-shaped compound

Many of Jamestown's early woes were due to the inability of the new colonists to meet the demanding nature of carving a home from the wilderness. The settlement party consisted primarily of "gentlemen," who had few or no skills and little experience in house construction, farming, fishing, and defense. This idealized scene quite accurately depicts an early construction project wherein a few are performing the work, while many watch.

From an old engraving in the author's collection.

and appropriately named it James Fort in honor of James I, the ruling monarch of England. By the end of the year, only thirty-five or so colonists remained in the infant town, the rest having perished from disease, the elements, or else from continued assaults by the unfriendly natives.

Three months after the Jamestown settlement got underway in earnest, other English colonists landed on the coast of present-day Maine, near the

When Englishmen arrived at the site of Jamestown in 1607, they found the surrounding territory settled by a large confederation of Indians made up of several distinct tribes and loosely controlled by a chief named Powhatan. The natives were agricultural in nature, and their villages consisted of their homes surrounded by fields of corn, tobacco, melons, and beans.

From *A Briefe and True Report of the New Found Land of Virginia,* by Thomas Harriot, Frankfurt, 1590.

mouth of the Kennebec River, and established the Crown's second outpost in the New World. Called Popham's Colony, after its founder, George Popham, this northern effort was sanctioned by the Virginia Company of Plymouth and consisted of about one hundred prospective settlers. By winter, all but forty-five people had perished. Following the death of Popham and a grueling first year, the survivors evacuated the colony during the next autumn.

1608

Christopher Newport left Jamestown soon after the fort was completed. His mission was to proceed to England and to recruit new settlers. Upon his return to Virginia in January, 1608, he found the town in ill repair with very few of the residents able to perform physical labor.

In Jamestown, Anne Burras, the maid to Mrs. Thomas Forest, married John Laydon, a laborer, in the first Christian marriage in America.

Captain John Smith, who had accompanied Newport with the original 1607 colonization effort, was elected president of the Jamestown colony.

Early Jamestown residents conferring with local Indians, while other tribesmen work on a dugout canoe.

Painting by Carl Rakeman, courtesy of the Federal Highway Administration.

Although he served for only about one year, Smith provided the dysfunctional colony with the sorely needed leadership ("He who does not work, will not eat") necessary to survive.

1609

The Virginia Company of London's second charter was issued, providing structure for company officials to appoint the Virginia colony's governor who would have "full and absolute power and authority to correct, punish, pardon, governe [sic] and rule." The nebulous boundaries of the colony were also vastly extended to include a significant portion of the present-day United States.

In August, seven ships carrying four hundred new colonists arrived at Jamestown.

After suffering severe burns from a gunpowder explosion, John Smith left Jamestown and returned to England in October. He never returned to Virginia.

Captain John Smith, who was elected president of the Jamestown colony in 1608, is pictured threatening Powhatan's brother, Opechancanough. When the Indian refused to trade with Smith for corn, he "did . . . take this murdering Opechancanough . . . by the long lock of his head and with my pistol at his breast" persuaded the native to load his boat with twenty tons of corn.

From *The Generall Historie of Virginia, New England, and the Summer Isles,* by John Smith, London, 1624.

1610

The Virginia colony's population stood at 350 residents.

The winter of 1609-10 presented serious challenges to Jamestown and its citizens. The trying period witnessed a famine that accounted for the deaths of close to ninety percent of the colony's residents. The few survivors were relegated to eating "Hogges, Dogges, and horses . . . together with rats, mice, snakes or what vermin or carrion soever we could light on . . . ." Of the horrible event, John Smith later lamented, "This was that time, which still to this day we called the starving time: it were too vile to say, and scarce to be beleeved, what we endured."

Sir Thomas Gates, the new lieutenant governor, arrived at Jamestown in May. Distressed at the town's pitiful condition, he resolved to move its residents to Newfoundland and eventually to England. The following month, as Gates and his followers sailed down the James River toward the sea, they were met by Governor Thomas West (Lord De La Warr) and ordered to return to their abandoned homes. With an iron hand, De La Warr took control of the colony, and, by the time he left for the West Indies the next year, he had partially restored Jamestown to its earlier, healthier condition.

1611

Health issues forced Governor De La War to vacate Jamestown in March. In the meantime, Lieutenant Governor Gates had returned to England for supplies, provisions, and more colonists. In May, a new deputy governor, Thomas Dale, along with three hundred new settlers, arrived at Jamestown. Within one month, Dale, concerned that the town and its inhabitants were virtually defenseless against either Indian or foreign attack, invoked martial law.

1612

When Jamestown's first English colonists arrived in 1607, they discovered that local natives smoked a form of tobacco that they grew in their village gardens. Although the Englishmen were familiar with tobacco – the plant was imported to the island nation around 1565 and smoking had become so commonplace by 1604 that King James had condemned the habit – that grown by the Indians was different. One colonist complained that the native tobacco was "not of the best kind, it is but poore and weake, and of a byting tast . . . ." John Rolfe began experimenting with other varieties of tobacco attempting to find a blend to satisfy the tastes of

Detail from John Smith's Map of Virginia, *showing the region around Jamestown. The inset depicts Powhatan surrounded by his tribesmen.*

From *A Map of Virginia, With a Description of the Country, the Commodities, People, Government and Religion,* by John Smith. London, 1612.

Pocahontas, the daughter of the Indian chief, Powhatan, married John Rolfe at the newly constructed church in Jamestown in 1614.

From an old engraving in the author's collection.

all good Englishmen. Rolfe imported Spanish tobaccos from Trinidad and South America and mixed them with the locally grown product. Before long, he had developed a variety that "no doubt but after a little more triall and expense in the curing thereof. . .will compare with the best in the West Indies."

The Virginia Company of London proclaimed its third and final charter in March. The document remained valid until 1624, when Virginia became a royal colony under the control of the Crown.

John Smith published his book entitled, *A Map of Virginia, With a Description of the Country, the Commodities, People, Government and Religion.* The book and the map that accompanied it were based on his personal observations and notes made in Virginia during his earlier sojourn. Over the next few years, Smith's map would often be relied upon by adventurers to America.

1613

During the year, 1613, affairs in Jamestown deteriorated, primarily because of renewed Indian hostility. As a defense, Pocahontas, the daughter of the powerful chief Powhatan, was captured and held hostage until the Indians ceased their warring activities. In the meantime, Pocahontas and the Englishman, John Rolfe, who had advanced the economy of the colony by the introduction of tobacco, fell in love.

1614

Thomas Dale, who had been succeeded as deputy governor by Lieutenant Governor Thomas Gates in 1611, reassumed control of Jamestown in March, reporting directly to Governor De La Warr *in absentia.*

Pocahontas accepted Christianity and was baptized with the name Rebecca. She and John Rolfe were wed at Jamestown in April, thus providing a measure of peace between the Indians and the colonists.

1615

Pocahontas bore John Rolfe a male child whom the couple named Thomas.

A True Discourse of the Present Estate of Virginia, written by Ralph Hamor, a former secretary of the colony, was published in London.

1616

Thomas Dale was succeeded as deputy governor by George Yeardley. The successful policies initiated by Dale were soon forgotten, and Jamestown residents, so enamored by the potential of tobacco as a cash crop, began planting seedlings in every possible location – the streets, open places, and yards. Entire families went underfed because of the obsession with growing tobacco instead of food crops. During the year, a total of twenty-three hundred pounds of tobacco were exported to England.

The entire Rolfe family – John, Pocahontas, and baby Thomas – departed for England for a visit. While there, they had an audience with King James I and Queen Anne.

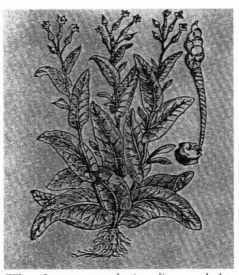

When Jamestown colonists discovered that growing tobacco profited them far more than other agricultural produce, they dedicated every available space in the village to the plant. As early as 1617, a visitor remarked that he "found the marketplace, and streets, and all other spare places planted with tobacco." Sadly, this mad lust for profit and the refusal to grow food crops nearly resulted in the starvation of many settlers.

From *Stirpium Adversaria Nova,* by Petrus Pena and Matthias de L'Obel, London, 1571.

1617

While sailing for the East India Company, Captain Christopher Newport, the commander of the original Jamestown expedition of 1607, died in Java and was buried at sea.

In March, while making plans with her family to depart from England for Jamestown, twenty-two year old Pocahontas suddenly took ill and died. She was buried at Gravesend. John Rolfe returned home alone.

1618

John Rolfe's earlier tobacco experimentation paid off quickly. When the colonists discovered that a good tobacco crop was worth up to six times more than any other agricultural commodity they could grow, tobacco culture mushroomed. This year, more than forty thousand pounds of tobacco were shipped from Jamestown to England.

Governor De La Warr died in June.

Pocahontas, John Rolfe, and their child, Thomas, were well accepted in England. Taking the Christian name, Lady Rebecca, she is shown in this 1616 engraving attired in typical English fashion of the times.

From *The Generall Historie of Virginia, New England, and the Summer Isles,* by John Smith, London, 1624.

Chief Powhatan, the father of Pocahontas died. He was a visionary who in the early 1570s had consolidated thirty regional Algonquian groups consisting of some thirteen thousand individuals into a single, six-thousand-square-mile chiefdom.

1619

George Yeardley, knighted the previous year by King James I, returned to Virginia in April as governor. He brought with him the Virginia Company's latest charter which called for the creation of a formal legislature and provided for the ownership of private land. The Virginia Assembly met for the first time in late July through early August at Jamestown. Delegates represented the major plantations located along the James River.

In August, a Dutch ship called on Jamestown, and by the time it left, Governor Yeardley and Abraham Peirsey had procured about twenty African slaves from the ship's captain in exchange for badly needed provisions.

Far upstream from Jamestown, an iron furnace – the first ever built in English America – opened for business on Falling Creek, a tributary of the James River just south of present-day Richmond. It was destroyed by an Indian raid during the massacre of 1622.

1620

Virginia's colonial population grew to 2,200 people.

The provision in the Virginia Company's latest charter that related to private land ownership was immediately popular to the colony's residents. Citizens who had lived there for three years prior to 1616 were awarded one hundred acres of land. Those who had arrived after 1616 and who had paid their own passage received fifty acres. The post-1616 arrivals whose expenses had been borne by the Company were required to serve as tenants on Company property for a period of seven years before being qualified for free land. John Rolfe was quick to see the results of the land giveaway, writing in

Jamestown is a hubbub of activity in this village scene dating to about 1620. The palisades to the fort and the James River are visible in the background.

Painting by Carl Rakeman, courtesy of the Federal Highway Administration.

1620 that the policy gave all recipients "greate content for now knowing their owne landes, they strive and are prepared to build houses & to cleere their groundes ready to plant, which giveth . . . greate incouragement, and the greatest hope to make the Colony florrish that ever yet happened to them."

1621

In July, it was determined "by authoritie directed . . . from His Majestie under his Great Seale," that two separate councils be established to improve government in the Virginia colony. The "Counsell of State" was to consist of individuals selected by the Company, while the "Generall Assembly" was to be filled with two burgesses from each town and plantation in the colony.

Although glassmaking in Virginia was begun by a few Germans and Poles in 1608 "in the woods neere a myle from James Towne," it got underway seriously this year when six Italian glassblowers disembarked at Jamestown.

1622

When Powhatan died in 1618, he was succeeded by a brother, Opitchapam, who proved to be an ineffective leader. He was replaced by

The entire Virginia colony was practically wiped out in 1622 when Powhatan's brother and successor, Opechancanough, launched an attack on most of the plantations in the region. Hundreds of settlers were killed, and much property damage was suffered.

From an old engraving in the author's collection.

another brother, Opechancanough, who lived up to the standards for his tribe set by Powhatan. Peace between the colonists and the local Indians had been an on-again, off-again affair since the days of first settlement. By the early 1620s, however, relations between the two peoples had again become strained. In March, Opechancanough launched an all-out attack on the Virginia colony, and his warriors struck plantation after plantation up and down the James River. More than three hundred Virginians were killed. Governor Francis Wyatt declared martial law. English refugees from all over the eastern seaboard used Jamestown as a gathering point, and the sudden increase in the town's population severely strained its food reserves. Among those plantations that have been scientifically studied in light of the extensive Indian attacks is Martin's Hundred, located on the grounds of today's Carter's Grove Plantation.

1623

The devastating effects of the great Indian uprising of the previous nine months were still being felt as the new year opened. Then, as if the isolated colonists had not suffered enough, they were struck with the dreaded disease, plague, accompanied by another famine. According to one contemporary observer, the plague accounted for twice as many fatalities as the Indian war had. More hundreds died as Virginia Company officials in London watched their investments evaporate. Finally, in April, Opechancanough declared that "blud enough had already been shedd on both sides," and asked for a truce. Several prisoners were exchanged and gradually planters returned to their plantations to pick up the pieces of their shattered lives.

1624

Reacting to the many adverse reports that seemed to be reaching him in increasing numbers, King James I revoked the Virginia Company's charter in May. Thus, with a stroke of the pen, Virginia passed from a private enterprise to a royal colony. The Company's bold experiment had lasted only seventeen years.

John Smith published his book, *The Generall Historie of Virginia, New-England, and the Summer Isles,* in London.

1625

The new council, operating under the authority of the Crown, met at Jamestown in April. Francis Wyatt, who had served as governor for the Virginia Company since 1621, was kept in office under the new regime. The council consisted of Francis West, George Yeardley, George Sandys, Roger

Smyth, Ralph Hamor, John Martin, John Harvey, Samuel Mathews, Abraham Peirsey, Isaac Maddison, and William Claiborne.

In London, King James I, after a reign of twenty-two years, died and was succeeded by his twenty-five year old son, Charles I. Among other things, James is remembered for his role in the establishment of the New World English settlements at Jamestown and Plymouth, the 1611 publication of the King James Version of the Holy Bible, and the execution of Sir Walter Raleigh.

1626

George Yeardley was again appointed governor of Virginia, replacing Francis Wyatt. William Claiborne, a twenty-five year old planter, was named secretary of state, the colony's number two position.

In September, Governor Yeardley presided over a witchcraft trial at Jamestown. The defendant was Goodwife Wright of nearby Kecoughtan Plantation. She was accused of a variety of crimes, including responsibility for the deaths of a child, a neighbor, and a number of chickens.

1627

During the spring, Secretary William Claiborne and a small following explored the waters of Chesapeake Bay in order to "discover any rivers or Creeks within the Bay up to the heads of the same and trade with the Indians for Corne Skins or any other Comodities whatsoever." The real purpose of the mission was to make sure that the Bay and all of its natural resources fell under control of the Virginia colony and not some future interloper. The trip also provided Claiborne with valuable experience in dealing with the natives in the vast region.

Governor George Yeardley died in November and was succeeded by Francis West.

1628

The colony's first General Assembly operating under the authority of the Crown met at Jamestown in March. For the next several years, it would meet at least once a year to consider Virginia's progress, problems, and welfare.

1629

George Calvert, the first Lord Baltimore, along with his family, visited Jamestown to discuss with officials the founding of a new colony, but one that would lay within the boundaries of Virginia. He was met with antagonism and belligerence. Calvert had previously explored present-day Newfoundland as a potential settlement site, but the cold climate there drove him to the Chesapeake Bay area.

Dr. John Pott succeeded Francis West as governor. He instituted the regular holding of monthly courts, a concept which became the forerunner of the county court system.

1630

Virginia's colonial population reached 2,500.

At the end of his first year as governor, John Pott was replaced by John Harvey, who immediately brought charges against Pott for killing his neighbor's pigs. Harvey was resented by Jamestown residents, but apparently wielded enough influence to serve as governor for five years.

1631

William Claiborne established a trading post on Kent Island in the Potomac River. During the next few years, the island was incorporated into the new colony of Maryland.

1632

The General Assembly adopted the name, "Grand Assembly," and called itself by that name until 1680. From the tone of legislation passed, obvious concerns centered on the importance of tobacco in the colony's economy, defense from neighboring Indians, and religious matters.

1633

Still sensitive to recurring native hostility and remembering the terrible massacre of 1622, colonists built a picketed stockade connecting the James and York Rivers. Indians were prohibited from entering the cordoned-off area.

In February, the establishment of Middle Plantation, later to be renamed Williamsburg, was authorized.

1634

Designating institutions that had already been a part of England's heritage for many years, Virginia officials divided the colony into eight "shires" or counties: James City, Henrico, Charles City, Elizabeth City, Warrascoyack (changed to Isle of Wight in 1637), Charles River, Warwick River, and Accomac (spelled without a "k"). The office of sheriff, the shire's highest ranking government official, was also created.

In March, Leonard Calvert, brother of Cecilius Calvert, the second Lord Baltimore, landed several hundred shipmates in Virginia territory along the northern bank of the Potomac River. The new arrivals established the town of St. Mary's, which became the first settlement in a new colony called Maryland. The colonization project had begun with the Calvert brothers' father, George, the first Lord Baltimore. Remarkably, Calvert was able to wrest a charter from Charles I that not only allowed his heirs to be "true and absolute lords and proprietaries" of the new colony, but one that gave refuge and protection to English Catholics who had suffered at home at the hands of the predominant Anglican Church.

1635

Thomas Rolfe, the twenty-year-old son of Pocahontas and John Rolfe, returned to Jamestown to claim his inheritance.

The unpopular governor, John Harvey, was arrested and charged with treason by members of his own Council. John West was in turn elected governor by the Council to serve "until his majesty's pleasure be known."

1636

New Norfolk County (now extinct) was created from Elizabeth City County.

1637

Upper Norfolk and Lower Norfolk Counties (now extinct) were created from New Norfolk County.

Former Governor John Harvey, back in good graces with the king, returned to Jamestown and resumed his previous role. He arrested those responsible for his earlier ouster and shipped them all to England to answer to the Crown.

1638

Early on in Jamestown's settlement, the raising of silk worms became an exciting possibility for the colonists. Unfortunately, many of the local insects they believed to be silkworms were actually common caterpillars. Nevertheless, silkworm culture and the production of mulberry trees to support the insect continued to be explored. The Assembly renewed this interest by suggesting that a new look be taken at the industry's potential.

For a brief time, Virginians believed that the production of silk would bring them the financial success that tobacco had. Officials back home in England also eyed the development of the silk industry with interest, since the only other source of the desirable cloth was far-away and inaccessible China. Unfortunately, silk worms were not native to the New World and the imported stock did not thrive well. An additional problem was the inability for the colonists to appreciate the complexity of making silk, one step of which is shown here.

From *Virginia's Discovery of Silke-Wormes,* by Edward Williams. London, 1650.

1639

Governor Harvey failed to come to terms with his Virginia subjects and they again expelled him. This time, he was replaced by Francis Wyatt, who had already served as governor on two different occasions.

A new church at Jamestown was begun.

1640

Virginia's colonial population reached 10,442.

1641

Virginia planters exported 1,300,000 pounds of tobacco at an average price of two pence per pound.

1642

William Berkeley arrived in Jamestown in February to replace Francis Wyatt. Berkeley quickly put an end to the internal dissention in the colony and soon gained the support of most of Virginia's residents.

1643

Accomac County's name was changed to Northampton County. Charles River County was renamed York County. Warwick River County was renamed Warwick County (now extinct).

The Grand Assembly passed laws requiring all church services to follow the disciplines of the Church of England. Ministers who violated the acts were subject to expulsion. In other legislation, the Assembly modified the monthly court system of government established in 1629; now the courts would be called "county" courts and would convene every other month.

1644

During April, members of the Pamunkey Indian Federation under the leadership of Opechancanough attacked several outlying plantations and killed nearly five hundred colonists. In retaliation, the Assembly ordered the colonists to "pursue and root out those [Indians] which have any way had theire hands in the shedding of our blood and massacring of our people." Governor Berkeley departed Jamestown for England in June, his mission to appeal to the Crown for aid in combating the natives. Richard Kemp served as acting governor during Berkeley's absence.

1645

In order to improve the colony's defenses, the Assembly ordered the construction of three forts to be placed at the fall lines of the James (Fort Charles), Pamunkey (Fort Royal), and Chickahominy (Fort James) Rivers. The poll tax was temporarily removed, and the colony's county courts were authorized to try all common law and equity cases.

William Berkeley returned to Jamestown and resumed his role as governor.

1646

The Assembly authorized the placement of another stockade, Fort Henry, at the falls of the Appomattox River.

Opechancanough was captured by colonists, imprisoned at Jamestown, and eventually assassinated by one of his guards. Peace was made with the ancient warrior's successor, Necotowance, in October. A new era dawned for

After orchestrating yet another terrible attack upon Virginia settlers in 1644, the old warrior Opechancanough was captured two years later, imprisoned at Jamestown, and killed by a guard. He was believed to have been around one hundred years old.

Courtesy of the U. S. National Park Service.

Virginia with the signing of the peace. No longer, on paper at least, were the Indian neighbors of the colonists to be treated like a "perpetual enmity," but were to have their own rights of land ownership.

1647

When they were apprised of a rumor that Parliament had suspended Dutch trading privileges with Virginia, Assembly members condemned the story, declaring that "wee conceive [it] to bee the invention of some English merchants on purpose to affright and expel the Dutch, and make way for themselves to monopolize not onely our labours and fortunes, but even our persons." The Assembly quickly reaffirmed the right of Dutch traders to ply their wares among Virginia's colonists.

1648

Northumberland County was created from previously unorganized land lying between the Potomac and Rappahannock Rivers.

Boats and other water craft must have been relatively common in early Virginia. In a book entitled *A Perfect Description of Virginia*, published in 1648, the author revealed that there existed "pinnaces, barks, great and small boats many hundreds, for most of their plantations stand upon the rivers' sides and up little creeks and but a small way into the land."

1649

King Charles I of England was beheaded by his foes in Parliament on January 30. When members of the Virginia Assembly learned of Charles's death later in the year, they bemoaned "the late most excellent and now undoubtedly sainted king" and promised to prosecute any person who defended "the late traitorous proceedings." Likewise, charges of treason would be brought against anyone who questioned the right of Charles II to succeed his late father. However, Charles was not succeeded by his son, but by Oliver Cromwell, who ruled not as king, but as "Lord General of the Commonwealth." Cromwell was a minor member of Parliament and, after his death in 1658, he was followed by his inept son.

During Oliver Cromwell's interregnum, the English Parliament dispatched a fleet to Jamestown to assure that Virginia colonists supported Cromwell and desisted from entertaining the succession of Charles II, son of the beheaded King Charles I.

From an old engraving in the author's collection.

1650

Virginia's colonial population reached 18,731.

The second edition of E. W. Gent's book, *Virginia: More especially the South part thereof, Richly and truly valued*, was published in London. The new printing contained a great deal of information, particularly on the subjects of silkworm culture, winemaking, and timber and lumber usage.

In August, on the assumption that a way to the Pacific Ocean (thought to be merely a few miles away) could be found, Governor William Berkeley sent Edward Bland and Abraham Wood on an expedition from Fort Henry that eventually carried the adventurers across the present-day North Carolina border as far south as the region lying between the Roanoke and Tar Rivers. When they returned home eight days later, they were "all well and in good health," despite the fact that they "every night kept a strickt watch, having our Swords girt, and our Guns and Pistols by us, for the Indians every night where we lay, kept a strict guard upon us."

Parliament, sitting in London and concerned with the pro-Crown attitudes of Virginia's residents and government, threatened to blockade the colony's sea trade.

1651

Gloucester County was created from York County, and Lancaster County was created from Northumberland and York Counties.

Members of Virginia's Assembly defied Parliament and its blockade threat.

In London, Edward Bland published *The Discovery of New Brittaine*, an account of his previous year's expedition in Virginia.

1652

Surry County was created from James City County.

Following more ominous threats, this time from a sizeable English fleet lying offshore at Jamestown, Governor William Berkeley retired from office and

Title-page from Edward Bland's book detailing his exploratory journeys in Virginia in 1650.

From *The Discovery of New Brittaine*, by Edward Bland. London, 1651.

An early scene at the Jamestown wharf.

Drawing by Sidney E. King. Courtesy of the U. S. National Park Service.

was succeeded by Richard Bennett. The Virginia colony was now under the control of Parliament, and for the next eight years, its governors were elected by the General Assembly.

1653

Westmoreland County was created from Northumberland County.

George Hacke, a physician and native of Cologne, Germany, migrated to Northumberland County. He became a naturalized citizen, and, before he died, he had acquired a several-thousand acre plantation and assembled an extensive library of books.

1654

New Kent County was created from York County.

Each county court was empowered with the authority to nominate its respective county sheriff.

1655

Edward Digges was elected governor by the Assembly, replacing Richard Bennett.

The right to vote was restricted to "housekeepers [people who maintained houses] whether freeholders, leaseholders, or otherwise tenants." The law was extremely unpopular.

1656

The original Rappahannock County was created from Lancaster County. It became extinct in 1692.

The previous year's legislation regarding voting rights was amended when Assembly members interpreted the restriction as "something hard and unagreeable." They failed to reason how "any persons shall pay equall taxes and yet have no votes in elections." All freemen, whether housekeeper or not, were thence given the right to vote. Authority was also given to the county courts to nominate justices of the peace.

Samuel Mathews, Jr. became governor, replacing Edward Digges.

George Washington's great-grandfather, John, arrived in Virginia from England.

1657

Edward Nott, Virginia's governor from August, 1705-August, 1706, was born.

1658

A statement to John Gosling, a York County resident, from Dr. John Clulo revealed that a physician's services in early Virginia were quite valuable indeed. For professional services rendered to Gosling – which included "an astringent potion," a "purging potion," and a "cordial julep" – Dr. Clulo charged nearly five hundred pounds of tobacco.

In England, Oliver Cromwell died and was succeeded by his son, Richard.

1659

Governor Mathews informed the Assembly of the death of Oliver Cromwell and the succession of his son. The Assembly, in turn, gave its endorsement of Richard Cromwell's appointment.

1660

The Virginia colony's population soared to more than 27,000 residents.

Governor Mathews died in January and was succeeded by William Berkeley.

Charles II, son of the beheaded Charles I, ascended to the English throne in May, ending the eleven-year interim government by Oliver Cromwell and his son, Richard. News of the event reached Virginia in September.

1661

In an impassioned plea, an anonymous writer known only as "R. G." implored the bishop of London to advocate more centralized infrastructure in Virginia. He reasoned that, since most residents lived "at such distances from each other" and that "many of them are very remote from the house of God," they suffered from an absence of religious and educational opportunity.

The number of burgesses per county was increased to two.

1662

Accomack (spelled with a "k") County was created from Northampton County.

The Assembly passed legislation favorable to boat and ship builders. One act declared that "every one that shall build a small vessel with a deck be allowed, if above twenty and under fifty tons, fifty pounds of tobacco per ton; if above fifty and under one hundred tons, one hundred pounds of tobacco per ton; if above one hundred tons, two hundred pounds per ton. Provided the vessel is not sold except to an inhabitant of this country in three years."

Another act passed by the Assembly required that all future buildings be constructed of brick in order to diminish the danger of fire.

1663

Indentured servants of Gloucester County, weary of their seemingly unending allegiance to their masters, plotted an insurrection, but one of their own revealed the scheme. He was given his freedom afterwards. Years later, a novel entitled *Prisoners of Hope*, by Mary Johnston, was inspired by the incident.

1664

Stafford County was created from Westmoreland County.

1665

The Grand Assembly passed an act prohibiting arms and ammunition sales to the Indians.

The first recorded theatrical presentation in the New World was given at Fowkes' Tavern in Accomack County. Entitled "The Bear and the Cub," the performance brought charges against its three producers "for acting a play."

1666

Robert Hunter and George Hamilton, both future governors of Virginia who never visited the colony, were born.

1667

The new year entered and proceeded with ominous signs for the residents of Jamestown. In April, a severe storm hit, bringing with it "haile . . . as big as turkey eggs." In June, a small Dutch flotilla raided and burned several tobacco ships moored at Newport News and captured thirteen English merchant ships. During late August, "the most dreadful hurry cane that ever the colony groaned under" struck Jamestown and environs, destroying much of the precious tobacco crop.

1668

The average size of a land grant in Virginia was 890 acres.

1669

Middlesex County was created from Lancaster County.

1670

Virginia's colonial population stood at 35,309.

John Lederer, a young German-born physician, was commissioned by Virginia's governor, William Berkeley, to explore the backwoods wilderness of the colony beyond the Fall Line. Lederer, accompanied by three Indians, left the village of Chickahominy in early March and a few days later reached the headwaters of the South Anna River. The following day, Lederer reached the divide of the Blue Ridge Mountains northeast of present-day Charlottesville and exclaimed, "The fourteenth of March, from the top of an eminent hill, I first descried the Applataean Mountains, bearing due West to the place I stood upon . . . ."

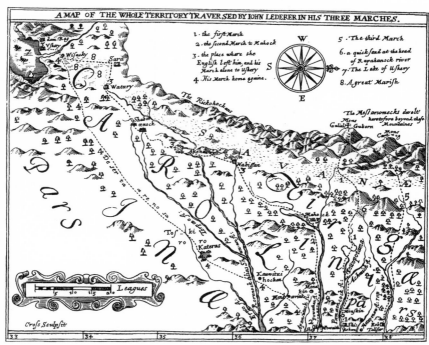

John Lederer's map depicting his travels from the village of Chickahominy to the Blue Ridge Mountains in 1670.

From *The Discoveries of John Lederer In Three Several Marches from Virginia, to the West of Carolina,* by John Lederer. London, 1672.

1671

African-Americans, serving as both slaves and as indentured servants, represented about five per cent of Virginia's colonial population.

In September, Captain Abraham Wood, a resident of Fort Henry (present-day Petersburg) commissioned an expedition to explore the trans-Allegheny Mountains region with the goal of "finding out the ebbing & flowing of the Waters on the other side of the Mountains in order to the discovery of the South Sea." The party, led by Thomas Batts, Thomas Woods, and Robert Fallam (or Fallows), crossed the mountains near Adney Gap. Near the present-day West Virginia-Kentucky boundary line, they blazed a tree with Governor Berkeley's initials. When the group returned in October, they declared, "God's holy name be praised for our preservation."

1672

In London, John Lederer's book, *The Discoveries of John Lederer, In Three Several Marches from Virginia, to the West of Carolina*, was published. It recounted his 1670 Blue Ridge Mountains expedition.

1673

Abraham Wood, still intent on finding the "South Sea," sent yet another expedition into the Virginia wilderness. Led by James Needham and Gabriel Arthur, the exploring party left Fort Henry and traveled southward across present-day North Carolina and into Georgia. Needham was eventually killed by Indians near the North Carolina-South Carolina border. Arthur continued the journey, spending the winter of 1673-74 with Cherokee Indians "in a strange land, where never English man before had set foote, in all likelihood either slaine, or att least never likely to return to see the face of an English man," today's East Tennessee.

1674

Twenty-seven year old, Cambridge-educated Nathaniel Bacon, Jr., the nephew of Nathaniel Bacon, Sr. and a cousin by marriage to Governor William Berkeley, arrived in Virginia. He soon purchased a large tobacco plantation and accepted a seat on the Council.

1675

Indian troubles flared up again along the Chesapeake Bay frontier. The Virginia militia under the command of Colonel George Mason and Captain George Brent chased the natives into Maryland.

1676

In a short-lived rebellion that occurred in eastern Virginia, the colony's primary town at Jamestown was destroyed by fire in September. The culprits were followers of Nathaniel Bacon, Jr., who had repeatedly tried to persuade the governor, William Berkeley, to provide his region of Virginia with protection from the Indians. Berkeley steadfastly refused aid, and Bacon took matters into his own hands, massacring a number of Occaneechi Indians even though the tribe was friendly. When the governor refused to sign a commission making Bacon the commander-in-chief, an honor already bestowed upon him by the Assembly, Bacon torched Jamestown. When Bacon succumbed to "lice and flux" later in the year at Gloucester, the revolt soon died as well. Governor Berkeley began a series of ruthless executions that lasted into the following year.

Followers of the rebellious Nathaniel Bacon, Jr. presenting their demands to Governor William Berkeley at the statehouse in Jamestown.

From an old engraving in the author's collection.

1677

Among those Virginians executed by Governor Berkeley for their participation in Bacon's Rebellion were Thomas Young, Henry Page, Thomas Hall, William Drummond, John Baptista, James Crews, William Cookson, John Digbie, Giles Bland, Anthony Arnold, John Isles, Richard Pomfrey, John Whitson, and William Scarburgh, all hanged between January and March.

After the carnage of Bacon's Rebellion and its bloody aftermath were over, Governor Berkeley was ordered by King Charles II to return to England. Colonel Herbert Jeffreys was appointed lieutenant governor. Berkeley was an ill man when he departed Jamestown in April, and he died in July.

Thomas Culpeper was soon named the new governor to succeed William Berkeley, although he did not arrive in Virginia until May, 1680. In his absence, Jeffreys, the appointed lieutenant governor, ran the colony until his death the following year.

1678

Henry Chicheley, the deputy governor, assumed the governor's office in December, upon the death of Jeffreys.

1679

The issues of property and fishing rights gained importance as the region around Jamestown and its outlying area continued to grow. Robert Liny, a landowner, complained to the Grand Assembly that although he "had cleared a fishing place in the river against his own land to his great cost and charge supposing the right thereof in himself by virtue of his patents, yet nevertheless several persons have frequently obstructed him in his just privilege of fishing there, and despite of him came upon his land and hauled their seines on shore to his great prejudice."

1680

The Virginia colony's population reached nearly 44,000.

The Assembly passed legislation that "there be in every respective county fifty acres of land purchased by each county and laid out for a town and storehouses." The act's purpose was to provide what the Assembly called "trading towns," to which plantation owners could conveniently carry their produce, especially

A flurry of building activity occurred in the Virginia colony when the Assembly passed legislation requiring the establishment of "trading towns," which were designed to serve as focal points for the collection of goods and produce for export.

Drawing by Sidney E. King. Courtesy of the U. S. National Park Service.

tobacco, for export. Among the towns established at the time were Henrico, Surry, James City, Elizabeth City, York, Gloucester, and Lancaster.

1681

In London, Morgan Godwin published his book, *A Supplement to the Negro's & Indians Advocate: or, Some Further Considerations and Proposals for the Effectual and Speedy Carrying of the Negro's Christianity in our Plantations.* The twelve page pamphlet provided additional comment to Godwin's earlier book in which he advocated the baptism of slaves and Indians as well as their admission into the Church.

1682

King Charles II urged Governor Culpeper to expand his Virginia colony with new development and the creation of new towns. Jamestown, now three-quarters of a century old and "not only the most antient but the most convenient place for ye Metropolis of our said Colonie," was recommended to be rebuilt.

1683

Governor Culpeper was relieved of his gubernatorial duties. He was temporarily succeeded by Nicholas Spencer, the president of the Council. Upon his arrival in Jamestown the following year, Francis Howard assumed the governor's role.

1684

Following Bacon's Rebellion and the burning of Jamestown, the Assembly was required to meet wherever it could, using local taverns and residences whenever possible. Finally, Colonel Philip Ludwell was hired to rebuild the statehouse.

1685

Reverend John Clayton, who was also a Jamestown physician, left an interesting account of his treatment for hydrophobia, the dreaded condition left from the bite of a rabid dog. "I told them, if anything in the world would save his life," he wrote, "I judged it might be the former vomit of volatile salts." Continuing, he reported, "They ran away and left me, saying, he [the affected man] was now certainly a dead man . . . . Nevertheless it pleased God that he shortly after cried, *this fellow in the black has done me good,* and after the first vomit, came so to himself, as to know us all."

1686

The Virginia colony discontinued the use of its protective "Ranger" force. The Rangers had been organized several years earlier as an irregular military unit that "ranged" the woods and remote outlying areas far from the colony's towns and plantations.

1687

On October 21, amidst "the beat of the drum and the firing of two great guns and with all the joyfulness this colony is capable to express," the Council announced to Jamestown residents King James II's "Declaration for Liberty of Conscience." The declaration legalized non-Anglican religious activity.

1688

In England, King James II was deposed.

1689

The successors to King James II were his daughter, twenty-seven-year-old Queen Mary II, and her husband, thirty-nine-year-old King William III, of Holland.

1690

Virginia's colonial population passed the 50,000 mark for the first time.

1691

King and Queen County was created from New Kent County. Norfolk County (now extinct) was organized from Lower Norfolk County, as was Princess Anne County (now extinct).

All former acts and regulations dealing with the Indian trade were repealed and a policy of "free and open trade for all persons at all times and at all places with the Indians whatsoever" replaced them.

A "Port Act" created the city of Yorktown. The Crown confirmed Jamestown as Virginia's capital and urged all Council members to obtain land grants and build houses upon them.

1692

Essex and Richmond Counties were created from the old Rappahannock County.

Edmund Andros became governor.

It was a happy day for the residents of Middle Plantation when construction began on the College of William and Mary during the summer of 1695. Thomas Hadley, an English master craftsman, supervised the laying of the foundation to the original building, thought to be designed by Sir Christopher Wren.

From *The Book of Trades, or Library of the Useful Arts,*
published by Jacob Johnson. Richmond, Virginia, 1807.

1693

A charter was enacted in February approving the creation at Middle Plantation (today's Williamsburg) of the College of William and Mary, named in honor of the reigning sovereigns. The new school would provide "a certain place of universal study, or perpetual college, for divinity, philosophy, languages and other good arts and sciences." James Blair was appointed president and Henry Compton, the bishop of London, was bestowed the chancellor's chair.

1694

Reverend James Blair, the new president of William and Mary, assumed a position on the Council. In the future, the vocal churchman would be a constant source of irritation to successive governors and Council members.

1695

During the 1670s, when the Dutch threatened Jamestown from the sea, a brick fort had been constructed to protect the town. Now the structure was in bad need of repair, but the Council deemed it less expensive to raze the fortification and replace it with a new one. John Tullett, a local craftsman was hired to level the fort, while another worker was commissioned to build "a platform for the great guns."

Construction began at the College of William and Mary. The original structure, the Wren Building, was reputedly designed by the famed English architect, Sir Christopher Wren. Today, it is the oldest academic building still in use in America.

1696

A law was passed by the Assembly which provided Virginia clergymen with an annual salary of sixteen thousand pounds of tobacco.

1697

Reverend James Blair, the new president of William and Mary and a perennial critic of the local government, had little praise for the newly completed fort at Jamestown. In a letter to English officials, he wrote that the governor had "thrown away a great deal of money in [razing] an old fort at Jamestown, & in building a powder house, and in making a platform for 16 great guns there."

1698

Francis Nicholson, a former Virginia lieutenant governor and most recently the governor of Maryland, replaced Edmund Andros as governor at Jamestown.

During October, a disastrous fire destroyed the statehouse at Jamestown, presenting an opportunity to consider another site as the colony's capital.

As the end of the seventeenth century rapidly approached, the nearly one-hundred-year-old town at Jamestown fell on hard times. After fire destroyed the statehouse in 1698 and support grew for the removal of the colony's capital to Middle Plantation, only a few residents remained behind to work their small fields.

Drawing by Sidney E. King.
Courtesy of the U. S. National Park Service.

1699

As the seventeenth century came to a close, Jamestown contained about thirty houses and several hundred residents. Governor Nicholson complained, however, that the town was "reduced to so mean a condition that it cannot give entertainment to the people attending both a General Assembly and a General Court together."

Governor Nicholson and the Council decreed that all official business pertaining to the colony would, beginning the following year, be conducted at Williamsburg, the new name for Middle Plantation.

1700

Virginia's colonial population approached 59,000 people.

About 170 French Huguenots landed at Jamestown, intending to establish a colony several miles up the James River.

Graduation ceremonies at William and Mary were attended by many visitors, including some from Pennsylvania and New York, as well as by a delegation of friendly neighboring Indians who observed the proceedings with great interest.

The Assembly held its December session at the newly opened College of William and Mary in Williamsburg.

1701

King William County was created from King and Queen County.

In an effort to rapidly populate the outer reaches of the region with settlers, the Assembly passed an act calling for the "better strengthening of the frontiers."

1702

Prince George County was created from Charles City County.

During a ceremony at William and Mary celebrating the succession of Queen Anne, Governor Nicholson and the college president, James Blair, vigorously bantered with each other, resulting in a permanent rift between the two men.

The primary building at the College of William and Mary as it appeared in 1702.

From *Report of the Journey of Francois Louis Michel from Berne, Switzerland, to Virginia.* Reprinted in *Virginia Magazine of History,* Richmond, Virginia, 1916.

1703

Some Council members, supported by the large plantation owners of the region, demanded that Governor Nicholson be recalled. The governor's supporters included the clergy, who in turn attacked James Blair, Nicholson's foremost critic.

Queen Anne advised officials at the new capital that it was her desire to maintain Virginia's seat of government at Jamestown. Replying that neither she nor her predecessors had ever vetoed the law moving the capital to Williamsburg in the first place, they continued construction on the new capitol building.

1704

In what is perhaps the earliest instance of preparations being made for an anniversary of Jamestown's original settlement, Governor Nicholson announced plans for a centennial celebration for the year, 1707. His recall in 1705, however, ended such ambitions.

1705

By this year, according to a list published by the Assembly, twenty ferries operated across the James River and its tributaries, twenty more across the York River and its tributaries, eight more across the Rappahannock River, one across the Potomac, and two to the Eastern Shore.

Robert Beverley's *The History and Present State of Virginia,* was published in London.

A law enacted by the House of Burgesses relegated all black slaves to "personal property" status, meaning that they could be bought and sold at the pleasure of their owners. American Indians also lost many of their previously gained legal privileges, among them the right to testify in court.

The Capitol at Williamsburg was completed.

1706

In April, while still trying to grapple with the low price of tobacco, Virginia plantation owners exported three hundred ships full of the plant.

1707

Parliament in London passed the Act of Union, whereby the previously independent entities of England and Scotland became known collectively as Great Britain.

In order to get their tobacco to the warehouse for inspection and to port for shipping abroad, Virginia farmers utilized what were known as "tobacco-rolling" roads. After the tobacco was placed in large casks, similar to today's fifty-five gallon oil drums, the kegs were attached to a team of oxen and pulled along the road, usually accompanied by a few slaves who oversaw the operation. One road connected northern Virginia with Richmond, while two others in the south linked Petersburg with North Carolina and Mecklenburg County with Petersburg.

Painting by Carl Rakeman, courtesy of the Federal Highway Administration.

1708

The Assembly passed legislation to take effect on December 25, detailing the fees that port authorities could charge for the individual ownership of vessels.

1709

The Virginia colony exported twenty-nine million pounds of tobacco at an average price of one pence per pound, exceeding all previous records.

1710

Virginia's colonial population approached the 80,000 mark.
The Governor's Palace in Williamsburg was completed.

Bruton Parish Church in Williamsburg as it appeared in the early part of the eighteenth century.

Painting by Alfred Wordsworth Thompson.

1711

The vestry of Bruton Parish Church in Williamsburg approved plans for rebuilding the sanctuary, which was in a "ruinous" state. After renovation, the church, which dated back to 1674, was described by a visitor as "nicely regular and convenient, and adorned as the best Churches in London."

1712

In an early example of property condemnation, the Assembly passed legislation allowing tobacco warehouses to be built at public expense, even on property that was privately held. Under the act, if the landowner refused to sell the parcel for the warehouse, the county government conducted a fair appraisal, condemned the land, purchased it, and built the structure. If the warehouse ever was de-commissioned, the property reverted to the previous owner.

1713

Lieutenant Governor Alexander Spotswood introduced an innovative inspection program whereby defective tobacco was eliminated from warehouses. Planters with marketable tobacco were issued receipts. Within three years, Spotswood's opposition had orchestrated the discontinuance of the program.

1714

Lieutenant Governor Spotswood devised a method whereby the surrounding Indian tribes would be separated into groups, with each group given a unique hunting preserve to be monitored by white officials. Several of the local tribal chiefs signed a treaty to this effect in February.

Concerned that the large supply of arms and ammunition recently given to the Virginia colony by Queen Anne would ruin if not better protected, Williamsburg officials decreed that "one good substantial House of Brick" be built to accommodate the valuable supplies. The Magazine, as the building became known, was built for some two hundred pounds sterling paid out of duty money collected on slaves and liquor.

Lieutenant Governor Spotswood built several iron furnaces on the Rapidan River. For manpower, Spotswood brought in German emigrants.

1715

Dismayed at the transfer of James County court functions from Jamestown to Williamsburg, a group of citizens petitioned the governor to relocate the court "at some other Place more convenient to the Inhabitants of the said County than the City of Williamsburg."

Thomas Walker – physician, burgess, land speculator, and discoverer of Cumberland Gap – was born in King and Queen County.

1716

During the summer, Lieutenant Governor Alexander Spotswood led an exploring party to the Blue Ridge Mountains in order to "encourage gentlemen to venture backwards and make discoveries and new settlements." One of Spotswood's follow-

Lieutenant Governor Alexander Spotswood and his men resting at the crest of the Blue Ridge Mountains during the 1716 expedition. After enjoying the view and a good dinner, one of the group, John Fontaine, a British army officer, wrote that "we got the men together, and loaded all their arms, and we drank the King's health in Champagne, and fired a volley, the Princess's health in Burgundy, and fired a volley, and all the rest of the Royal Family in claret, and a volley. We drank the Governor's health and fired another volley."

From an old engraving in the author's collection.

ers was John Fontaine, an English army officer, who later wrote that "We followed the windings of the James River, observing that it came from the very top of the mountains . . . . In some places it was very steep, in others, it was so that we could ride up . . . . [We] got to the top of the mountain . . . and we came to the very head of James River, where it runs no bigger than a man's arm."

William Levingston built a theater, the first in English North America, near the Palace in Williamsburg.

1717

Lieutenant Governor Spotswood's tobacco and Indian resolutions of 1713 and 1714 were vetoed by the Crown at the insistence of London merchants.

Edward Teach, better known as "Blackbeard," was killed and beheaded by members of a government-sponsored expedition from Williamsburg. Teach's head was placed on public display in the colonial capital.

From an old engraving in the author's collection.

1718

For some months, pirates led by Edward Teach, better known as "Blackbeard", had harassed shipping along the Atlantic coast. Accordingly, Lieutenant Governor Spotswood organized an expedition to ferret out the culprits and punish them. When Spotswood's men and Teach's pirates met, a Lieutenant Maynard severely wounded Blackbeard, who soon died. Maynard beheaded the pirate and brought his prize, along with several prisoners, back to Williamsburg where they were publicly displayed.

John Donelson, who opened up new territory for white settlement with "Donelson's Line" following the signing of the Treaty of Lochaber, was born. Donelson later co-founded Nashville, Tennessee, and his daughter, Rachel, married Andrew Jackson.

1719

Like some of his predecessors, Lieutenant Governor Spotswood had problems with the Reverend James Blair. In May, in a letter to the Lords of Trade, Spotswood reported that affairs between the two men continued to deteriorate.

1720

Virginia's colonial population increased to nearly 88,000 residents.

Brunswick, Hanover, and King George Counties were created from Prince George, New Kent, and Richmond Counties respectively. Spotsylvania County was created from parts of Essex, King William, and King and Queen Counties.

1721

Peyton Randolph – King's attorney for Virginia, burgess, and president of the Continental Congress – was born in Williamsburg.

1722

In July, the status of Williamsburg was changed by charter from a "town" to a "city."

During the last days of his administration, Lieutenant Governor Alexander Spotswood and the Iroquois League of Nations signed a treaty forbidding the Indians from crossing the Blue Ridge Mountains or the Potomac River without express approval.

Hugh Drysdale succeeded Alexander Spotswood as lieutenant governor.

> The common Planters leading eafy Lives don't much admire Labour, or any manly Exercife, except Horfe-Racing, nor Diverfion, except Cock-Fighting, in which fome greatly delight. This eafy Way of Living, and the Heat of the Summer makes fome very lazy, who are then faid to be Climate-ftruck.
>
> The Saddle-Horfes, though not very large, are hardy, ftrong, and fleet; and will pace naturally and pleafantly at a prodigious Rate.
>
> They are fuch Lovers of Riding, that almoft every ordinary Perfon keeps a Horfe; and I have known fome fpend the Morning in ranging feveral Miles in the Woods to find and catch their Horfes only to ride two or three Miles to Church, to the Court-Houfe, or to a Horfe-Race, where they generally appoint to meet upon Bufinefs; and are more certain of finding thofe that they want to fpeak or deal with, than at their Home.

20 From Hugh Jones, *The Prefent State of Virginia*, London, 1724

Some comments about early Virginians written by Hugh Jones in his book, The Present State of Virginia.

From *The Present State of Virginia,* by Hugh Jones. London, 1724.

1723

Former Lieutenant Governor Spotswood established an iron smelting plant with an air furnace near Fredericksburg. The furnace used bituminous coal as fuel.

In the May session of the Assembly, legislation passed that taxed the importation of slaves, while at the same time ordering closer supervision of those slaves already living in Virginia. London merchants quickly persuaded the King to veto the law.

1724

The Present State of Virginia, by Hugh Jones, was published in London.

1725

George Mason – co-founder of Alexandria, long-time member of the House of Burgesses, Virginia legislator, and delegate to the Constitutional Convention of 1787 – was born in Fairfax.

1726

Benjamin Harrison – veteran burgess, speaker of the Virginia legislature, governor of Virginia, and member of the Virginia Ratification committee – was born in Charles City County. Harrison was the father of President of the United States, William Henry Harrison, and the great-grandfather of President Benjamin Harrison.

George Wythe – burgess, member of the Continental Congress, first law professor in the United States, delegate to the Constitutional Convention, and signer of the Declaration of Independence – was born near Black River in Elizabeth City County.

1727

Statutes for the College of William and Mary provided for an "Indian School" with one instructor, whose mission was "to teach the Indian boys to read, and write, and vulgar arithmetic." Additionally, "he [the schoolmaster] is to teach them thoroughly the catechism and the principles of the Christian religion." For these duties the teacher annually received between forty and fifty pounds sterling.

1728

Caroline County was created from parts of Essex, King and Queen, and King William Counties. Goochland County was created from Henrico County.

In February, as Virginians strayed further afield from the colony's original coastal settlements, the Assembly created the towns of Fredericksburg and Falmouth.

William Byrd II and other Virginia and Carolina commissioners surveyed the boundary line between the two colonies. In March, Byrd wrote that the wharf at Norfolk, founded nearly fifty years earlier, contained "more than 20 brigantines and sloops," adding that "the town is so near the sea that a vessel can sail in and out in a few hours."

Land grants were issued for the first time to prospective settlers of Virginia's Great Valley. The region soon became a haven for Scots-Irish and German immigrants.

1729

Neighboring Carolina had been chartered in 1663 by King Charles II to a group of eight friends and entrepreneurs, one of whom was Governor William Berkeley of Virginia. The colony was loosely divided into northern and southern parts, with the northern section being favored by Berkeley for potential settlement sites. This year, the governments of the two entities were officially divided into separate colonies: North Carolina and South Carolina.

1730

The Virginia colony's population soared to 114,000 residents.

Prince William County was created from parts of Stafford and King George Counties.

William Parks, formerly of Maryland, arrived in Williamsburg to fill the role of official printer for the Virginia colony. Six years later, he also edited the *Virginia Gazette*.

1731

Martha Dandridge, who in 1759 as a widow with two children would marry George Washington, was born in New Kent County.

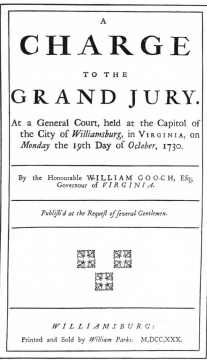

A

CHARGE

TO THE

GRAND JURY.

At a General Court, held at the Capitol of the City of *Williamsburg*, in VIRGINIA, on *Monday* the 19th Day of *October*, 1730.

By the Honourable WILLIAM GOOCH, Efq; Governour of *VIRGINIA*.

Publish'd at the Request of several Gentlemen.

WILLIAMSBURG:
Printed and Sold by *William Parks*. M,DCC,XXX.

Soon after his arrival in Williamsburg in 1730, William Parks printed several books of which this one, printed that same year, was one of the earliest.

From *A Charge to the Grand Jury At a General Court, held at the Capitol of the City of Williamsburg, in Virginia, on Monday the 19th Day of October, 1730*. Williamsburg, 1730.

1732

Richard Henry Lee – childhood friend of George Washington, burgess, member of the Continental Congress, and United States senator – was born in Westmoreland County. George Washington, first president of the United States, was born on Pope's Creek in Westmoreland County.

John Blair – burgess, delegate to the Constitutional Convention, and associate justice of the U. S. Supreme Court – was born in Williamsburg.

In late July, with the laying of the foundation, construction on the President's House on the campus of the College of William and Mary began.

1733

In London, a pamphlet entitled *The Case of the Planters in Virginia* which reproduced a petition issued the previous year by the House of Burgesses was published. John Randolph had been dispatched to England by the House in order to present the petition to Parliament. Basically, the document requested Parliament to restructure the tobacco market so that a more equitable profit could be realized by Virginia planters.

1734

Amelia County was created from parts of Prince George and Brunswick Counties. Orange County was created from Spotsylvania County.

Francis Lightfoot Lee – burgess, delegate to the Continental Congress, and signer of the Declaration of Independence – was born in Westmoreland County.

1735

John Adams, second president of the United States, was born in Braintree, Massachusetts. At the second Continental Congress in 1775, it was Adams who nominated George Washington as commander-in-chief of the Continental Army. When Washington was elected the nation's first president, Adams was elected as his vice president. Adams died in Massachusetts on July 4, 1826, fifty years to the day that the Declaration of Independence was promulgated and the same day on which Thomas Jefferson died in Virginia.

1736

Patrick Henry, called the "Firebrand of the Revolution," was born in Hanover County. With little formal education, Henry rose to become a lawyer, burgess, delegate to the Continental Congress, and the Commonwealth's first governor. In 1765, when he was accused of treason by fellow burgesses for decrying the Stamp Act, he retorted, "If this be treason make the most of it!"

Williamsburg printer, William Parks, published the first issue of *The Virginia Gazette.*

1737

William Byrd II and William Mayo laid out the future town of Richmond. Five years later, the town was actually established, and in 1779, it was named the capital of Virginia to become effective the following year.

1738

Augusta and Frederick Counties were created from Orange County.

1739

A French soldier on his way from Canada with a detachment of troops to fight the war with the Chickasaws discovered Big Bone Lick in present-day Boone County, Kentucky, then a part of western Virginia. The Lick was a depository for the bones of prehistoric animals and, at its height of popularity, drew the interest of scientists from all over the world.

1740

Virginia's colonial population reached nearly 181,000 people.

1741

Captain Lawrence Washington, George Washington's half-brother and favorite relative, was decorated by Admiral Edward Vernon for his valorous service against the Spanish fortress at Cartagena. When he returned to Virginia from the battle, Washington renamed his Hunting Creek plantation, Mount Vernon, in the admiral's honor.

1742

Fairfax and Louisa Counties were created from Prince William and Hanover Counties respectively.

The Compleat Housewife, by E. Smith, was published by William Parks in Williamsburg. It was the first cookbook ever published in the American colonies.

1743

Thomas Jefferson, third president of the United States, was born at Shadwell in today's Albemarle County, but which at the time was Goochland County.

During mid-century, two private speculative organizations, the Ohio Company and the Loyal Company, were granted several hundred thousand acres of untamed and unsettled land in southern and western Virginia. Several prominent Virginians were involved in both of the companies which sent surveyors into the wilderness to chart their new properties.

Painting by Carl Rakeman, courtesy of the Federal Highway Administration.

1744

Albemarle County was created from Goochland County.

1745

Lunenburg County was created from Brunswick County.

1746

During King George's War, Virginia officials dispatched 136 officers and men to Albany in New York to assist with the British invasion of Canada.

1747

The Ohio Company – initially consisting of a group of influential Virginians, including Thomas Lee, George Fairfax, and Augustine and Lawrence Washington, with George Washington, Governor Robert Dinwiddie, and George Mason joining later – was awarded a giant land grant of 200,000 acres along the Ohio River. The company's goal was to develop the land and to settle it with families.

The Capitol at Williamsburg was mysteriously destroyed by fire. "A most extraordinary Misfortune befel this Place, by the Destruction of our fine Capitol," exclaimed an article in *The Pennsylvania Gazette* datelined "Williamsburg. Feb. 5."

The Reverend William Stith published his book, *The History of the First Discovery and Settlement of Virginia*, with the Williamsburg printing firm of William Parks.

1748

Martha Wayles, who as a widow would marry Thomas Jefferson in 1772, was born in Charles City County.

1749

The Assembly granted the Ohio Company an additional 700,000 acres. In the meantime, in July, the Loyal Company, a competitor to the two-year old Ohio Company, was granted an 800,000 acre parcel that stretched to the western mountains along the Virginia-North Carolina border. The company, with Peter Jefferson, Dr. Thomas Walker, Edmund Pendleton, and Joshua Fry at the helm, was more speculative in nature than the Ohio Company and had little interest in domestic settlement.

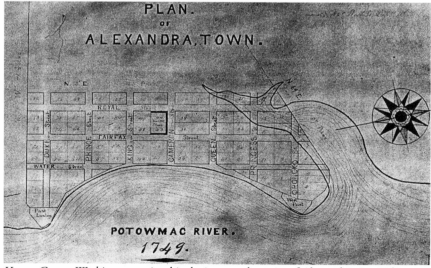

Young George Washington assisted in laying out the town of Alexandria in 1749.

Alexandria, situated on the upper Potomac River, was established. As a young surveyor, George Washington helped lay out the town.

Chesterfield, Culpeper, Cumberland, and Southampton Counties were created from Henrico, Orange, Goochland, and Isle of Wight Counties, respectively.

Washington and Lee University in Lexington was established as Augusta Academy. It was later renamed Washington Academy after George Washington who was a large donor to the school. Upon the death of its president, Robert E. Lee, in 1870, it changed its name again to Washington and Lee University.

The cost to repair the Capitol at Williamsburg was determined to be nearly 1,300 pounds sterling.

1750

Virginia's colonial population approached 231,000 residents.

Martha Dandridge married her first husband, Daniel Parke Custis. Before the death of Custis only seven years later, the couple had four children, two of whom, John and Martha, survived and witnessed their mother's marriage to George Washington in 1759.

Cumberland Gap as it appeared a few years after Dr. Thomas Walker discovered it in 1750.

From an old engraving after the drawing by Harry Finn in *Picturesque America*. New York, 1872.

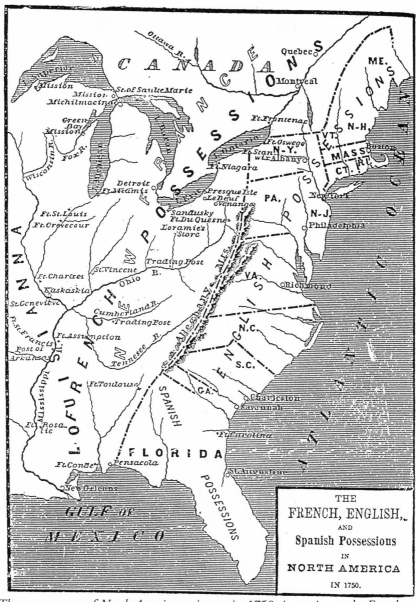

The eastern part of North America as it was in 1750, just prior to the French and Indian War. Basically, the British held the Atlantic seaboard and Piedmont regions, the French controlled the interior of the continent from the Gulf of Mexico through Canada, and Spain occupied Florida.

From *Historical Collections of the Great West*, by Henry Howe. New York, 1855.

Dr. Thomas Walker, one of the principals in the Loyal Company, left his plantation, Castle Hill in Albemarle County, in March to explore the western country. A month later, he spied a pass in the mountains which he named Cumberland Gap in honor of the Duke of Cumberland. The Wilderness Road which was eventually carved through the Gap became the highway along which thousands of Virginia and North Carolina emigrants sought their fortunes in the West.

1751

James Madison, fourth president of the United States, was born at Port Conway in King George County.

Carter's Grove, the magnificent plantation house of Carter Burwell, a grandson of Robert "King" Carter, was built along the James River in James City County.

1752

George Rogers Clark – Revolutionary War hero, conqueror of Vincennes and Kaskaskia, and older brother of William Clark – was born in Albemarle County.

Dinwiddie and Halifax Counties were created from Prince George and Lunenburg Counties respectively.

In early December, twenty-four-year-old William Byrd III hosted what may be the first Thoroughbred horse race in North America at his plantation near Gloucester. His recently imported horse named "Tryal" was bested in the four-mile race by a Maryland mare named "Selima."

1753

Bedford, Prince Edward, and Sussex Counties were created from Lunenburg, Amelia, and Surry Counties respectively.

Edmund Randolph – member of the Continental Congress, governor of Virginia, United States attorney general, and United States secretary of state – was born in Williamsburg.

Twenty-one year old George Washington, a major in the Virginia militia, was dispatched by Lieutenant Governor Robert Dinwiddie on a mission to inform the French commander of the Ohio valley that his forces must evacuate the region as soon as possible. On his way Washington stopped at the Forks of the Ohio River, today's Pittsburgh, and made the comment that the place was admirably suited for fortification. His observation was prophetic and soon the Forks did, indeed, become the site of, first a French fort and, a short time later, a British one.

1754

George Washington returned to Williamsburg from his mission to the French commandant with the disturbing news that the French had no intention of surrendering the rich Ohio River Valley. About three months later, Dinwiddie dispatched two military elements, one with orders to hastily build a fort at the Forks of the Ohio, and the other,

Raleigh Tavern in Williamsburg was a gathering place for the town's leading citizens as the French and Indian War drew nearer.

From an old engraving in the author's collection.

under the command of Washington, now a lieutenant-colonel, to cut a road through the Virginia, Maryland, and Pennsylvania wilderness and to provide support. Before the British fort could be completed, however, it was forced to surrender to the French. In the meantime, in backwoods Pennsylvania, Washington's small command had engaged a contingent of French soldiers who, after a short siege, demanded Washington's surrender. The inexperienced Washington had built a small stockade, which he named Fort Necessity, but on July 4, twenty-two years to the day before America's declaration of independence, he capitulated to the superior French forces. The brief encounter by the future "father" of the United States was the first battle of the French and Indian War.

William Hunter of Williamsburg published George Washington's account of his recent mission to the French commandant under the title, *The Journal of Major George Washington.*

1755

John Marshall – United States secretary of state and chief justice of the United States Supreme Court – was born in a part of Prince William County that four years later became Fauquier County.

Simon Kenton – Kentucky frontiersman, pioneer, and protégé of Daniel Boone – was born in Culpeper County.

General Edward Braddock, a sixty-year-old veteran of the elite Coldstream Guards, arrived at Hampton with two regiments of British infantry – the 44th and 48th – to assume command of all British and colonial military units in America. After moving his army to Alexandria, Braddock met with the governors of several colonies and mapped the strategy he would use to expel the French from North America. During the spring, the British troops left Alexandria. In July, following a grueling march through almost impenetrable forest, Braddock's redcoats and Virginians neared their destination, the French-held Fort Duquesne at the Forks of the Ohio River. Just a few miles from the fort, Braddock was mortally wounded in the vicious fighting that followed a bold ambush by the French and Indians. Braddock had four horses shot from beneath him before he was permanently disabled, and George Washington lost two animals. Sixty-three of the eighty-six British officers were killed or wounded, including all of Braddock's personal staff with the exception of Washington, who served as the general's personal aide. One thousand British and Virginia soldiers were either killed or wounded, while the enemy French and their Indian allies counted only fifty-six casualties.

ADVERTISEMENT.

A S it was thought adviseable by his Honour the Governor to have the following Account of my Proceedings to and from the French on Ohio, committed to Print; I think I can do no lef than apologize, in some Measure, for the numberlef Imperfections of it.

There intervened but one Day between my Arrival in Williamsburg, and the Time for the Council's Meeting, for me to prepare and transcribe, from the rough Minutes I had taken in my Travels, this Journal; the writing of which only was sufficient to employ me closely the whole Time; consequently admitted of no Leisure to consult of a new and proper Form to offer it in, or to correct or amend the Diction of the old; neither was I apprised, or did in the least conceive, when I wrote this for his Honour's Perusal, that it ever would be published, or even have more than a cursory Reading; till I was informed, at the Meeting of the present General Assembly, that it was already in the Press.

There is nothing can recommend it to the Public, but this. Those Things which came under the Notice of my own Observation, I have been explicit and just in a Recital of :——Those which I have gathered from Report, I have been particularly cautious not to augment, but collected the Opinions of the several Intelligencers, and selected from the whole, the most probable and consistent Account.

G. WASHINGTON.

George Washington's apologies for "the number of imperfections" in the account of his recent mission demanding French evacuation from the Ohio Valley were prominently displayed in his Journal, *published by Williamsburg printer, William Hunter.*

From *The Journal of Major George Washington, Sent by the Hon. Robert Dinwiddie, Esq; His Majesty's Lieutenant-Governor, and Commander in Chief of Virginia, to the Commandant of the French Forces on Ohio . . . ,* by George Washington. Williamsburg, 1754.

When the day was over, the British Army had suffered one of the worst defeats in its long history, and the future president of the United States found himself in temporary command of the remnant forces.

George Washington was promoted to commander-in-chief of all Virginia colonial troops.

1756

Henry "Lighthorse Harry" Lee – brilliant cavalry commander, member of the Continental Congress, governor of Virginia, and United States congressman – was born in Prince William County.

1757

Loudoun County was created from Fairfax County.

George Washington and Lieutenant Governor Robert Dinwiddie traveled to Philadelphia to attend a governors' meeting.

1758

A second Virginia militia unit, under the command of William Byrd III, was organized.

James Monroe, fifth president of the United States, was born in Westmoreland County.

George Washington and his Virginia troops, accompanied by British redcoats commanded by General John Forbes, visited abandoned Fort Duquesne, declared it to be occupied by the King's army, and renamed it Fort Pitt. Soon afterwards, Washington retired from the Virginia militia with ambitions of becoming a planter.

George Washington as he appeared during the French and Indian War. This is the earliest known portrait of Washington.

From an engraving after a 1772 painting by Charles Willson Peale.

1759

George Washington and Martha Dandridge married.

Fauquier County was created from Prince William County.

French dreams for a far-reaching American empire were dashed on September 13, when British army and naval forces led by General James Wolfe and Vice-admiral Sir Charles Saunders decisively defeated the French under the command of General Louis Joseph de Montcalm at Quebec in Canada.

1760

Virginia's colonial population reached nearly 340,000.

George III assumed the crown of Great Britain, ruling for the next fifty-nine years.

Seventeen-year-old Thomas Jefferson arrived in Williamsburg to attend the College of William and Mary.

1761

Amherst and Buckingham Counties were created from Albemarle County.

George Washington inherited his late half-brother Lawrence's Mount Vernon plantation.

1762

As the war in North America ended, France, rather than being forced to surrender its vast lands west of the Mississippi River to its arch-rival Great Britain, instead ceded the territory called Louisiana to Spain. This was the same expanse of land that President Thomas Jefferson would eventually purchase for the United States.

1763

The French and Indian War formally ended. Peace between Great Britain and France was signed at Paris.

In a futile attempt to contain the land-hungry American colonists, King George III announced his decision to declare all territory west of the crest of the Appalachian Mountains off-limits to settlement. Henceforth the territory would be "reserved under sovereignty, protection, and dominance of the King." Before the news ever reached America, however, the law had been broken, and pioneers by the thousands poured into the rich lands of Tennessee, Kentucky, and the Ohio River Valley. George Washington himself was not exempt from participating in the giant land grab. He instructed his land agent "to secure some of the most valuable lands in the King's part, which I

> And whereas it is juft and reafonable, and effential to Our Intereft and the Security of Our Colonies, that the feveral Nations or Tribes of *Indians*, with whom We are connected, and who live under Our Protection, fhould not be molefted or difturbed in the Poffeffion of fuch Parts of Our Dominions and Territories as, not having been ceded to, or purchafed by Us, are referved to them, or any of them, as their Hunting Grounds ; We do therefore, with the Advice of Our Privy Council, declare it to be Our Royal Will and Pleafure, that no Governor or Commander in Chief in any of Our Colonies of *Quebec*, *Eaft Florida*, or *Weft Florida*, do prefume, upon any Pretence whatever, to grant Warrants of Survey, or pafs any Patents for Lands beyond the Bounds of their refpective Governments, as defcribed in their Commiffions ; as alfo, that no Governor or Commander in Chief in any of Our other Colonies or Plantations in *America*, do prefume, for the prefent, and until Our further Pleafure be known, to grant Warrants of Survey, or pafs Patents for any Lands beyond the Heads or Sources of any of the Rivers which fall into the *Atlantick* Ocean from the Weft and North Weft, or upon any Lands whatever, which, not having been ceded to, or purchafed by Us as aforefaid, are referved to the faid *Indians*, or any of them.
>
> And We do further declare it to be Our Royal Will and Pleafure, for the prefent as aforefaid, to referve under Our Sovereignty, Protection, and Dominion, for the Ufe of the faid *Indians*, all the Lands and Territories not included within the Limits of Our faid Three New Governments, or within the Limits of the Territory granted to the *Hudfon's Bay* Company, as alfo all the Lands and Territories lying to the Weftward of the Sources of the Rivers which fall into the Sea from the Weft and North Weft, as aforefaid ; and We do hereby ftrictly forbid, on Pain of Our Difpleafure, all Our loving Subjects from making any Purchafes or Settlements whatever, or taking Poffeffion of any of the Lands above referved, without Our efpecial Leave and Licence for that Purpofe firft obtained.

King George's Proclamation of October 7, 1763 forbade colonial settlement west of the crest of the Appalachian Mountain chain in order to provide permanent hunting grounds for the indigenous Indian tribes in the vast region.

Courtesy of the Library of Congress.

think may be accomplished after a while, notwithstanding the proclamation that restrains it at present, and prohibits the settling of them at all."

1764

Charlotte and Mecklenburg Counties were created from Lunenburg County.

1765

At age seventeen, Martha Wayles, the future Mrs. Thomas Jefferson, married her first husband, Bathurst Skelton, who died within two years of the wedding.

Patrick Henry's 1765 address to his fellow Virginians in protest of the Stamp Act.

From an old engraving in the author's collection.

During a spirited speech before the House of Burgesses in protest of Great Britain's imposition of the Stamp Act, Patrick Henry was interrupted with cries of "Treason." The angry Henry continued, "Caesar had his Brutus, Charles the First had his Cromwell, and George the Third may profit from their example. If this be treason, make the most of it."

1766

Pittsylvania County was created from Halifax County.

John Overton – supervisor of the federal excise in President George Washington's administration, judge on the Tennessee Superior Court of Law and Equity, President Andrew Jackson's campaign manager, and co-founder of Memphis – was born in Louisa County.

1767

Rachel Donelson, daughter of John Donelson and future wife of Andrew Jackson, was born in Halifax County.

1768

In May, port authorities at Accomack allowed the schooner, *Anne*, commanded by William Wainhouse of New York, to unload its wares consisting of two boxes of chocolate, six barrels of cordial, three cases and two half-barrels of rum, six cases and one barrel of loaf sugar, one quarter-box of glass, one barrel of molasses, and eight hundred pounds of ham.

1769

Botetourt County was created from Augusta County.

1770

The Virginia colony's population neared the one-half million mark with 447,016 residents.

William Clark, who in 1805, along with Meriwether Lewis, fulfilled President Thomas Jefferson's dream of reaching the Pacific Ocean, was born in Caroline County.

An act to establish a public hospital at Williamsburg was enacted.

1771

John Murray, Earl of Dunmore, became Virginia's last colonial governor.

The March 15 issue of the *Virginia Gazette* revealed that "Yesterday was married, in Henrico, Mr. William Carter, aged 23, to Mrs. Sarah Ellyson, Relict of Mr. Gerald Ellyson, deceased, aged 85, a sprightly old Tit, with three Thousand Pounds Fortune."

1772

Shenandoah County was created from Frederick County. It was originally called Dunmore County, but the name was changed in 1778.

Thomas Jefferson, father of the Declaration of Independence.

From a print by Desnoyers. From *The American Revolution: A Picture Sourcebook.* Dover Publications, Inc. New York, 1975.

Martha Wayles Skelton and Thomas Jefferson married. The couple would have a son and five daughters, but only two of the children attained adulthood.

1773

Alexandria's Christ Church was completed at a cost of nearly $4,100. George Washington purchased a pew for $100.

William Henry Harrison, ninth president of the United States, was born at Berkeley in Charles City County.

In October, James Boone, son of the frontiersman, Daniel Boone, was killed by Shawnee Indians in present-day Lee County, forcing the elder Boone to suspend his Kentucky settlement efforts.

1774

Meriwether Lewis, captain of the 1805 Lewis and Clark Expedition to the Pacific Ocean, was born in Albemarle County.

A short time after residents of Boston staged their infamous "tea party," Yorktown's Collector of Revenue, Richard Ambler, led a similar foray against the ship *Virginia*, moored in the York River, and destroyed its cargo of tea.

As affairs between the Crown and the American colonies became more strained, Richard Henry Lee called for the formation of a Continental Congress to address the issues. A convention of Virginians selected Lee and fellow residents Peyton Randolph, George Washington, Patrick Henry, Richard Bland, Benjamin Harrison, and Edmund Pendleton to represent the colony at the Congress.

Bloodshed on the western frontier prompted Governor John Murray, Earl of Dunmore, to assemble some three thousand men to combat the restless Shawnee Indians. In October, at the confluence of the

As the American colonies moved nearer revolution, the British press had a field-day. In this satirical cartoon entitled, The Alternative of Williamsburg, *Virginia loyalists and patriots argue the next steps to be taken as war clouds loom. The loyalists are represented by the well-dressed in the crowd, while the patriots are content with homespun attire.*

From a 1775 London newspaper.

Thomas Jefferson purchased Rockbridge County's Natural Bridge and 157 surrounding acres in 1774 for "twenty shillings of good and lawful money."

From an old engraving in the author's collection.

Kanawha and Ohio Rivers, the two sides met in what has become known as the Battle of Point Pleasant, the only major conflict in "Lord Dunmore's War." The colonial army bested the Shawnees, who, under the command of their chief, Cornstalk, were forced to relinquish most tribal territory south of the Ohio River.

1775

Daniel Boone set out from the Long Island of the Holston River (present-day Kingsport, Tennessee) on his quest to blaze a trail through Cumberland Gap to the site of Boonesborough, Kentucky. The Trace eventually became known as the Wilderness Road, and thousands of emigrants used it to lead them to new lands and new lives in the West.

Patrick Henry delivered his "Give me liberty or give me death" speech at St. John's Church in Richmond.

Governor Dunmore confiscated all weaponry, ammunition, and powder from the Magazine at Williamsburg. Patrick Henry, leading the Hanover Independent Company of militia, halted a potential attack upon the governor when Dunmore begrudgingly released 330 pounds sterling in payment. Dunmore and his family then fled Williamsburg aboard the *H. M. S. Fowey*, moored in the York River.

The "shot heard around the world" was fired by British redcoats at Lexington, Massachusetts in April and from that point, Americans prepared themselves for the unavoidable war. Twenty-one days later, George Washington accepted command of the Continental Army.

1776

The British burned Norfolk.

Henry County was created from Pittsylvania County. Montgomery and Washington Counties were created from Fincastle County.

This broadside printed in Williamsburg made local citizens aware of the recent events during the battles at Concord and Lexington, Massachusetts.

From the author's collection.

Washington was the first county in the United States to be named in George Washington's honor. Today, counties in thirty-one states take their name from the first president.

Presbyterians established Hampden-Sydney College in Prince Edward County. The school was named in honor of John Hampden and Algernon Sydney, seventeenth century English libertarians. James Madison and Patrick Henry were among the school's first trustees.

In June, Patrick Henry was selected to become the Commonwealth of Virginia's first governor.

In July, American delegates to the Continental Congress declared "the United Colonies free and independent States." The Declaration of Independence, authored by Thomas Jefferson, was signed by John Hancock, the Congress's president, and Charles Thomson, the secretary, on July 4.

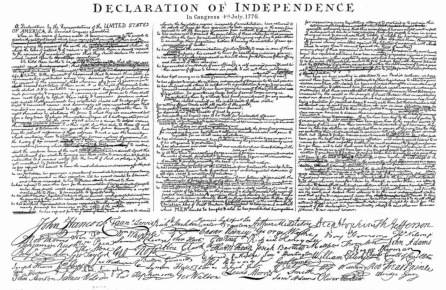

The original draft of the Declaration of Independence, the brainchild of Virginian Thomas Jefferson.

From *The American Revolution: A Picture Sourcebook.* Dover Publications, Inc. New York, 1975.

The rest of the delegates signed the document on August 2. The signers' names were kept confidential for six months in fear that they might be executed by the British if independence was not forthcoming.

The first collegiate social fraternity in America, Phi Beta Kappa, was established at the College of William and Mary.

1777

An excerpt from the *Journals of the Continental Congress* reported that "It being represented to Congress, that profaneness in general, and particularly cursing and swearing, shamefully prevails in the army of the United States, it is therefore Resolved, That General Washington be informed of this, and that he be requested to take the most proper measures, in concert with his general officers, for reforming this abuse."

Fluvanna and Powhatan Counties were created from Albemarle and Cumberland Counties respectively.

Henry Clay, noted Kentucky statesman who spent his first twenty years in Virginia, was born in Hanover County.

The Continental Congress, meeting at York, Pennsylvania, adopted the Articles of Confederation which brought the states into a union of individual governments working for the welfare of the whole.

General George Washington took his army into winter camp at Valley Forge, Pennsylvania. Before the next spring brought relief, three thousand American soldiers – "without clothes to cover their nakedness, without blankets to lie on, without shoes for want of which their marches might be traced by blood from their feet" – had died from lack of food, medical supplies, and warm clothing.

The Manufacturing Society of Williamsburg offered employment in the weaving industry to youthful black boys and girls although they were required to retain their "slave" status.

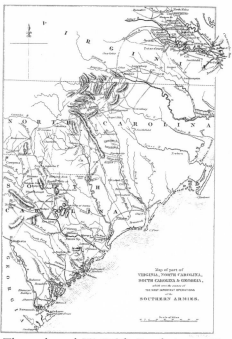

The southern theater in the Revolutionary War, depicting locations and actions in Virginia, the Carolinas, and Georgia.

From the author's collection.

1778

Rockbridge County was created from Augusta and Botetourt Counties. Rockingham County was created from Augusta County.

William Henry Ashley — lieutenant governor of Missouri, brigadier general of the Missouri militia, U. S. congressman, and the man who developed the "rendezvous" system of supplying remotely stationed Rocky Mountain fur traders with supplies and equipment in exchange for their furs — was born in Chesterfield County.

1779

Thomas Jefferson succeeded Patrick Henry as Virginia's governor.

The College of William and Mary attained university status by instituting separate schools of law, medicine, and modern languages.

1780

Virginia's population passed the one-half million mark.

The capital of the Commonwealth was moved from Williamsburg to Richmond.

Greensville County was created from Brunswick County.

1781

Campbell County was created from Bedford County.

In June, Jack Jouett, afterwards called the "Paul Revere of Virginia," made his famous ride to Charlottesville to warn Virginia officials of the approach of the British cavalry under the command of Lieutenant Colonel Banastre Tarleton.

After occupying Yorktown for two and one-half months, the British army, under the command of General Lord Charles Cornwallis, surrendered to George Washington and his French allies. "I request a cessation of hostilities for twenty-four hours to settle terms for surrender," the weary Cornwallis wrote to Washington. On October 19, to the tune of "The World Turned Upside Down," the defeated British army marched out of Yorktown and stacked arms. For all intent and purposes, the Revolutionary War was over.

The siege at Yorktown during October, 1781.

From *The American Revolution: A Picture Sourcebook.*
Dover Publications, Inc. New York, 1975.

1782

After suffering ill health for a number of years, Martha Jefferson died, leaving her husband, Thomas, a widower until his death forty-four years later.

*The British surrender at Yorktown in October, 1781. George Washington observes from
horseback as General Benjamin Lincoln accepts the sword from British Brigadier General
Charles O'Hara, who took the place of General Charles Cornwallis, the British commander
during the battle.*

Old engraving from a drawing by Felix O. C. Darley. From *The American Revolution:
A Picture Sourcebook*. Dover Publications, Inc. New York, 1975.

1783

In December, at New York City's Fraunces Tavern, George Washington
told his admiring fellow officers that "With a heart full of gratitude, I now
take leave of you." With those words, the hero of the Revolution forsook his
command of the Continental Army and retired to civilian life at Mount
Vernon.

The Peace of Paris – signed by the United States, Great Britain, France,
and Spain – officially ended the Revolutionary War.

In late December, the General Assembly ceded all of Virginia's land that
lay northwest of the Ohio River (the Old Northwest Territory, consisting of
today's states of Ohio, Indiana, Illinois, Michigan, and Wisconsin) to the
United States government "upon condition that the territory so ceded shall
be laid out and formed into states." When the deed to the vast region was
signed the following March, Thomas Jefferson headed a committee to
determine how the proposed states could best be formed. For the new entities
that might be organized, the imaginative Jefferson suggested such exotic names
as Metropotamia and Polypotamia.

Mount Vernon from the rear, as it appeared shortly after George Washington retired from the army to devote his life to that of a gentleman planter.

Old engraving from a painting by Charles Willson Peale.

1784

Zachary Taylor, twelfth president of the United States, was born in Orange County.

1785

Franklin County was created from Bedford and Henry Counties.

With George Washington at the helm, the Patowmack Company was organized with the goal of improving navigation on the Potomac River by the construction of a series of locks and canals.

Thomas Jefferson assumed the role of minister to France.

Notes on the State of Virginia, written by Thomas Jefferson in 1781-82, was first published anonymously in Paris. The following year, in London, the book was released in English and credited Jefferson with its authorship.

1786

Russell County was created from Washington County.

Winfield Scott, hero of the Mexican War and the first American to hold the army rank of lieutenant general since George Washington, was born in Dinwiddie County.

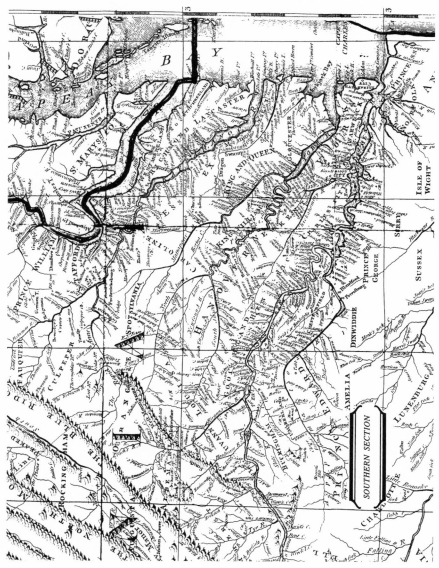

This map section, part of a larger map included in Thomas Jefferson's Notes on the State of Virginia, *was drawn by Joshua Fry and Peter Jefferson in 1751. It depicts astonishing detail, particularly with the rivers and streams, mountains, and villages and towns.*

Map of the Inhabited part of Virginia, containing the whole province of Maryland with Part of Pensilvania, New Jersey and North Carolina. London, 1751.

James Monroe and Elizabeth Kortright of New York City were wed and settled in Fredericksburg. The marriage produced two daughters and one son.

Virginia's General Assembly orchestrated a meeting with Maryland officials to discuss problems of mutual concern. Out of the gathering came the idea for a Constitutional Convention to be held the following year.

1787

In January, a huge fire destroyed fifty buildings in Richmond's business district, including the Byrd tobacco warehouse.

Plagued by a multitude of problems propagated by distance, social differences, and lifestyles, delegates from most of the thirteen states met in Philadelphia in May to attempt to stabilize the loosely written Articles of Confederation.

James Madison, whose keen insight into the political and human rights issues facing the infant United States inspired him to promulgate the Constitution.

From an engraving after the portrait by Gilbert Stuart. From *The American Revolution: A Picture Sourcebook.* Dover Publications, Inc. New York, 1975.

Failing in their original goal, the delegates, under the watchful eye of the Convention's chairman, George Washington, hammered out the Constitution, a comprehensive document that was the brainchild of James Madison. John Blair and James Madison represented the Commonwealth.

1788

Nottoway County was created from Amelia County.

In June, by a vote of eighty-nine "yeas" to seventy-nine "nays," the General Assembly, meeting in Richmond, ratified the Constitution, thereby making Virginia the tenth state to join the Union. All of the governmental functions recognized today were defined in the Constitution: the provision for a legislative branch of government with a bicameral Congress, the establishment of the executive branch and the definition of the duties and responsibilities of the president, and the vesting of legal matters with the judicial branch.

In conjunction with the ratification process, a few anti-federalist leaders including Patrick Henry and George Mason moved that a "Bill of Rights" be formulated to extend certain protections and rights to all Americans.

1789

Wythe County was created from Montgomery County.

George Washington was elected the new nation's first president.

President Washington proclaimed that November 26 be set aside as a day of thanksgiving for the Constitution which had become the law of the land by that time.

By the end of the 1780s, around one hundred Jews called Richmond home. There they organized the sixth synagogue in the United States and, at the time, the westernmost one. They called it Kahal Kadosh Beth Shalome.

1790

Virginia's population reached nearly three-quarters of a million residents.

Bath County was created from Augusta, Botetourt, and Greenbrier (in present-day West Virginia) Counties. Mathews and Patrick Counties were created from Gloucester and Henry Counties respectively.

John Tyler, tenth president of the United States, was born in Charles City County.

Letitia Christian, who married John Tyler in 1813, was born in New Kent County.

1791

In March, federal approval was given for the construction of the Cape Henry Lighthouse at the entrance of Chesapeake Bay. John McComb, Jr., a bricklayer from New York, was hired and urged to build a stone, octagonal building, "faced with hewn or hammer dressed Stone." The project was completed the following year at a cost of less than $18,000.

In December, the first ten amendments to the Constitution, called the Bill of Rights, the concept of which was originally proposed by members of the Virginia constitutional committee, were ratified by the Virginia Assembly. Since Virginia's ratification was the last required, the Bill of Rights became law.

1792

Grayson, Lee, and Madison Counties were created from Wythe, Russell, and Culpeper Counties respectively.

On June 1, the nine western Virginia counties located in the district of Kentucky were admitted to the union as an independent state known as the Commonwealth of Kentucky. The action followed Virginia's 1789 ruling allowing residents there to apply for statehood.

The Capitol in Richmond was completed, based on plans drawn by Thomas Jefferson.

1793

President George Washington's second inaugural address was the shortest in history. Consisting of only 133 words, the speech closed with "Previous to the execution of any official act of the President the Constitution requires an oath of office. This oath I am now about to take, and in your presence: That if it shall be found during my administration of the Government I have in any instance violated willingly or knowingly the injunctions thereof, I may (besides incurring constitutional punishment) be subject to the upbraidings of all who are now witness of the present solemn ceremony."

Two future heroes of Texas, Sam Houston and Stephen Austin, were born in Rockbridge and Wythe Counties respectively.

A Treatise on Gardening – the first gardening book ever published in Virginia and attributed to John Randolph of Williamsburg – was released by the printing press of T. Nicolson of Richmond. The book was read and recommended by Thomas Jefferson.

1794

James Madison married Dolley Payne Todd, a North Carolina widow with one child. The Madisons had no children between them.

1795

Congress authorized the establishment of a federal arsenal at Harpers Ferry (present-day West Virginia), making it the second oldest armory in the United States. President George Washington personally selected the site for the buildings, calling the place "the most eligible spot on the river."

1796

During mid-year, Francis Baily, a young Englishman who in later life became a founder and four-times president of the Royal Astronomical Society, paused in Norfolk during his journey to America. In his book, *Journal of a*

Tour in Unsettled Parts of North America in 1796 & 1797, he revealed that his room and board, which included breakfast and dinner, but no supper, cost one dollar per day. A typical breakfast, he wrote, consisted of "beefsteaks, sausages, stewed veal, fried ham, eggs, coffee and tea, and a dish, or rather a cake peculiar to the southern states, made out of the meal of Indian corn, and called hoe-cake, of which the inhabitants are very fond." Baily also commented on the popularity of billiards in the region, noting that he had discovered at least a dozen pool tables in Norfolk.

1797

As President George Washington neared completion of his two, four-year terms as president, he wrote a letter to Jonathan Trumbull, a poet and former law partner of John Adams. Washington declared, "Although I shall resign the chair of government without a single regret, or any desire to intermeddle in politics again, yet there are many of my compatriots (among whom be assured I place you) from whom I shall part sorrowing; because, unless I meet with them at Mount Vernon, it is not likely that I shall ever see them more."

1798

"I was born in Fredericksburg, Virginia, on the 26th of April, 1798." Thus begins Jim Beckwourth's autobiography, *The Life and Adventures of James P. Beckwourth*, published in New York in 1856. The noted mulatto mountain man and fur trapper who became a chief of the Crow Indians was the son of a Revolutionary War major and a slave.

1799

Tazewell County was created from parts of Wythe and Russell Counties.

In June, Patrick Henry, the man Thomas Jefferson credited as "far above all in maintaining the spirit of the Revolution," died at age sixty-three in Charlotte County.

George Washington died at Mount Vernon in December at the age of sixty-seven. His last words were "I find I am going . . . . I die hard but I am not afraid to go." To his attending physicians, he said, "I thank you for your attention, you had better not take any more trouble about me, but let me go off quietly."

1800

Virginia's population neared the 900,000 mark.

George Washington.

From an engraving after the portrait by
Rembrandt Peale. From *The American
Revolution: A Picture Sourcebook.* Dover
Publications, Inc. New York, 1975.

Martha Washington.

From *The American Revolution: A Picture
Sourcebook.* Dover Publications, Inc. New
York, 1975.

1801

President John Adams appointed John Marshall chief justice of the United States Supreme Court. He held the position until his death in 1835.

Thomas Jefferson was inaugurated third president of the United States. His previous career had included holding the positions of burgess, member of the Continental Congress, Virginia legislator, governor of Virginia, minister to France, U. S. secretary of state, and vice-president of the United States.

In May, a young student at the College of William and Mary, J. S. Watson, provided Virginia's earliest example of flight when he floated a hot-air balloon above the ground on the Court House Green. "I never saw so great and so universal delight as it gave to the spectators," Watson declared.

1802

Martha Washington, widow of George Washington, died in May at Mount Vernon at the age of seventy. She had survived her husband by only two and one-half years.

In July, Daniel Morgan – French and Indian War veteran, general during the Revolution, and large landowner in what later became West Virginia – died at Saratoga, his home in Winchester.

1803

In April, President Thomas Jefferson's twenty-year old dream came true when the United States purchased Louisiana from France for about three cents an acre. The previous January, Jefferson had already approached Congress for its approval to send an expedition consisting of "an intelligent officer with ten or twelve chosen men [who] might explore even to the Western ocean, have conferences with the natives on the subject of commercial intercourse, and return with the information acquired in the course of two summers." The congressional approval of the president's scheme signaled the beginning of the Lewis and Clark Expedition.

As Jefferson planned for the exploration of Louisiana, gunsmiths at the United States Arsenal at Harpers Ferry were busy putting the finishing touches on the U. S. Army Model 1803 rifle, the weapon that would eventually be carried by men of the Lewis and Clark Expedition.

1804

One of America's most famous mountain men, Jim Bridger, was born in March in Richmond. When he was eighteen years old, he went to work as a trapper for fellow Virginian, William H. Ashley, and his name was forevermore associated with the Rocky Mountain fur trade. Bridger is credited with the discovery of the Great Salt Lake, and, later in his career, he built Fort Bridger in present-day Wyoming as a resting and re-supply stop for emigrants traveling the Oregon Trail.

In mid-May, Virginians Meriwether Lewis and William Clark – accompanied by an assortment of American soldiers, French *engages,* Clark's slave, and one dog – left the wharf at St. Louis and slowly began their long journey to the Pacific Ocean and back. By cold weather, they had reached the villages of the Mandan Indians in present-day North Dakota, where they spent the winter.

1805

Men of the Lewis and Clark Expedition broke camp at the Mandan villages in April and began the second phase of their journey to the Pacific. If all went well they would arrive in the Oregon country before winter. With the expedition now were a young Shoshoni Indian woman named Sacagawea, her husband, and the couple's infant son, whom Lewis had helped deliver the previous February.

1806

Giles County was created from parts of Montgomery, Monroe (in present-day West Virginia), and Tazewell Counties.

Matthew Fontaine Maury, renowned oceanographer who would earn the name, "Pathfinder of the Seas," was born in Fredericksburg. When first released in 1855, his book, *The Physical Geography of the Sea*, was considered to be the "bible" of the relatively new science of oceanography.

1807

Nelson County was created from Amherst County.

Robert E. Lee – West Point graduate, superintendent of West Point, commander of the Army of Northern Virginia, and president of Washington College (present-day Washington and Lee University) was born in January in Westmoreland County. He was the son of "Light-Horse Harry" Lee.

Joseph E. Johnston – West Point graduate, topographical engineer, commander of the Army of Tennessee, and U. S. congressman from Virginia – was born in February in Farmville.

1808

Diomed, an English-imported stallion from whom generations of champion American thoroughbreds were descended, died at the age of thirty. He had been brought to Virginia in 1798 by Colonel John Hoomes of Bowling Green.

James Madison was elected fourth president of the United States to succeed his friend and neighbor, Thomas Jefferson.

1809

After serving two presidential terms, Thomas Jefferson retired to Monticello.

James Madison succeeded Jefferson as president.

In October, while on his way from St. Louis to Washington, D.C. to reconcile financial questions

Diomed, the English thoroughbred that sired dozens of American champion horses.

From *The Gentleman's New Pocket Farrier,* by Richard Mason. Philadelphia, 1853.

that had arisen during his governorship of Louisiana Territory, Meriwether Lewis mysteriously died – either by his own hand or by those of persons unknown – along the Natchez Trace in Tennessee.

1810

Virginia's population approached the 984,000 mark.

Joel Walker Sweeney, credited with the invention of the five-string banjo, was born near present-day Appomattox Court House.

1811

George Caleb Bingham, noted nineteenth century painter of the American West, was born in Augusta County. One of Bingham's most famous paintings, executed in 1851, is "Daniel Boone Escorting Settlers Through the Cumberland Gap."

On December, 26, 1811, the theater in Richmond in which Edgar Allan Poe's late mother had often performed was destroyed by fire. Mrs. Poe had only retired from the stage the previous month and had died on December 8. The tragic blaze killed seventy-one people and was thought to have begun when some of the scenery caught fire.

From *Historical Collections of Virginia,* by Henry Howe. Charleston, South Carolina, 1845.

1812

America's second war with Great Britain had its official beginning in June, when a reluctant U. S. Congress voted 79 to 49 in the House of Representatives and 19 to 13 in the Senate to declare war. A large factor in obtaining public support for the conflict occurred when a group of newly elected congressmen known as the "war hawks" – John C. Calhoun of South Carolina, Felix Grundy of Tennessee, and Henry Clay of Kentucky (Grundy and Clay were both born in Virginia) – vigorously protested Great Britain's policy of illegally seizing American seamen on the high seas.

1813

Edmund Randolph died in September in present-day Clarke County.

Virginian John Colter, sometimes called the "first" mountain man, died at his home in Missouri. Only thirty-eight years old at his death, Colter had accompanied Lewis and Clark to the Pacific Ocean during 1804-06. He left the expedition on the return home and went back to the Rocky Mountains where he became the first white man to view the wonders of present-day Yellowstone National Park.

1814

Scott County was created from parts of Lee, Russell, and Washington Counties.

In August, the British Army entered Washington, D. C. practically unhindered. Both the Capitol and the President's House were set ablaze and destroyed. President and Mrs. James Madison were forced to evacuate the city, but not before Dolley rescued the Declaration of Independence and the Gilbert Stuart portrait of George Washington.

This 1814 advertisement announced the fact that stage coach service between Richmond and Washington, D. C. was available every day rather than every other day as previously scheduled. A stage left each city at 3:00 A. M. and arrived at its destination fifteen hours later. The ad also promised to provide its customers with "the best and most pleasant of stages, good horses, & sober, steady, and skillful drivers."

From the author's collection.

In December, the War of 1812 was declared officially over with the signing of the Treaty of Ghent.

1815

John Sevier, first governor of Tennessee, died in Alabama. He was born in present-day Rockingham County and during his illustrious career he served as a soldier, Indian fighter, governor of the "lost" state of Franklin, and U. S. congressman.

1816

In February, the General Assembly passed an act "to create a fund for internal improvement" and to establish a public works authority, the first such organization in the United States. Loammi Baldwin was appointed the Commonwealth's engineer the following year.

George H. Thomas – Union army general, "the Rock of Chickamauga," and victor over the Confederacy at the decisive Battle of Nashville – was born in Southampton County in July.

Jubal A. Early – West Point graduate, Confederate general, participant in a multitude of campaigns fought on Virginia soil, and "unreconstructed" veteran – was born in Franklin County in November.

1817

James Monroe, the last of the "Virginia Dynasty" presidents, was inaugurated. His eight-year administration was known as "the era of good feeling."

1818

George Rogers Clark, scion of the famed Clark family of Virginia, died at his home in Louisville, Kentucky. Clark was an older brother of William Clark of the Lewis and Clark Expedition. During the Revolutionary War he had secured the Illinois country for the United States when he successfully routed the British from Kaskaskia.

1819

The General Assembly issued a charter to the University of Virginia in Charlottesville. The school, which actually opened its doors six years later, was the brainchild of Thomas Jefferson, who not only designed some of the buildings but also identified the first faculty and selected the first curriculum.

Many of the buildings at the University of Virginia in Charlottesville were designed by Thomas Jefferson, who also was influential in guiding the school during its formative years.

From *Historical Collections of Virginia,* by Henry Howe. Charleston, South Carolina, 1845.

1820

For the first time ever, Virginia's population surpassed the one million mark. This year's census also revealed that Virginia had fallen to second place in the Nation's population figures.

So far in America's history, only one non-Virginian, John Adams of Massachusetts, had been elected to the presidency. The other four – Washington, Jefferson, Madison, and Monroe – were all native-born Virginians. During this election year, John Adams's son, John Quincy Adams, the secretary of state in President Monroe's cabinet, threw his hat into the ring. When the electoral votes were counted, Monroe had garnered 231 of the 232 possible votes. The single dissenter was an elector who thought that no one other than George Washington should ever receive a unanimous vote.

1821

William Becknell, a native of Amherst County and lately a trader in Missouri, blazed a road across the southern Great Plains to New Mexico that became known as the Santa Fe Trail. Becknell's premier journey to the Southwest is considered the key event that assured a lucrative trade between American merchants and New Mexicans in the years prior to the Mexican War.

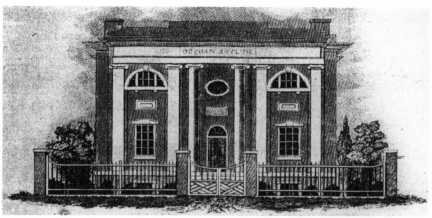

The Female Orphan Asylum in Norfolk as it appeared in 1819.

From an old engraving in the author's collection.

1822

Alleghany County was created from parts of Bath, Botetourt, and Monroe (in present-day West Virginia) Counties.

1823

In his annual message to Congress on December 2, President James Monroe put the world on notice that any foreign involvement in the political affairs of Western Hemisphere republics would be considered an assault upon the United States. This fundamental policy, known as the Monroe Doctrine, was rigidly enforced until the mid-twentieth century when Washington politicians looked the other way during the Communist takeover of Cuba.

1824

Thomas J. (Stonewall) Jackson – West Point graduate, Mexican War veteran, college professor, and corps commander in the Army of Northern Virginia – was born at Clarksburg (in present-day West Virginia). He died in May, 1863, from wounds received at Chancellorsville.

The Virginia House-wife, written by Virginia native Mary Randolph, was published by the firm of Davis and Force in Washington, D. C. The early cookbook contained recipes for a large variety of dishes, including such delicacies as catfish soup, roast calf's head, and broiled eels.

The Marquis de Lafayette, hero of the Revolution, visited Williamsburg where he was entertained at the Raleigh Tavern and in the home of Mrs. Mary Monroe Peachy.

Competing with the stage coach lines during the early and middle 1800s was the Chesapeake and Ohio Canal. Connecting Washington, D. C. with Cumberland, Maryland, the canal was officially begun in 1828 when President John Quincy Adams broke ground for it. Twenty-two years and eleven million dollars later, the canal finally reached Cumberland, via Harpers Ferry, only to soon lose its importance to the increasingly popular railroad.

From an old engraving in the author's collection.

1825

Less than nine months before he died at his home, Monticello, former president Thomas Jefferson consented to have a plaster cast made of his face. John Henri Isaac Browere began work on the project in October. The ordeal turned out to be more difficult and time-consuming than Jefferson had been led to believe. "Successive coats of thin grout plaister[ed] on the naked head, and kept there for an hour, would have been a severe trial for a young and hale person," the exhausted Jefferson exclaimed later.

A. P. (Ambrose Powell) Hill – West Point graduate, Mexican and Third Seminole Wars veteran, and corps commander in the Army of Northern Virginia – was born in Culpeper in November. Hill was killed in action in 1865.

1826

Thomas Jefferson died at Monticello on July 4, the fiftieth anniversary of the promulgation of the Declaration of Independence that he authored. Within hours of his death, fellow patriot and former president John Adams died at his home in Massachusetts.

1827

In order to access the markets in the territory northwest of the Ohio River, the General Assembly chartered the Northwestern Turnpike and authorized citizens of Winchester, Romney, Moorefield, Clarksburg, and other towns (some of which are located in present-day West Virginia) to help fund the project by purchasing stock.

While visiting the Williamsburg post office, a recently-arrived resident was more than impressed with his new home when he wrote, "I thought I was transported to Noah's Ark, when I first came into this Town, so prodigious was the Quantity of Animals I met with, without seeing a single Person until I reached the Post Office which stands in the Center of Main St. It is one of the Curiosities of this Place . . . . I will tell you that there is not Article whatever in the World which could not be found in it. It is a Book Seller's Store in which you will find Hams and French Brandy; it is an Apothecary's Shop in which you can provide yourself with black silk Stockings and shell Oysters; it is a Post Office in which you may have . . . chewing Tobacco & and in a Word it is a Museum of natural History in which we meet every Afternoon to dispute about the Presidential Election, and about the Quality of Irish Potatoes."

1828

On July 4, at a spot near the Powder Magazine at the Little Falls of the Potomac River, President John Quincy Adams dug his shovel into the hard ground and turned over the first dirt to be excavated for the Chesapeake and Ohio Canal. Approved three years previously, the canal cost investors fourteen million dollars before work was terminated at Cumberland, Maryland in 1850.

1829

Lott Cary, one of the founders of Liberia, died. Cary, the first black missionary to Africa, was born in 1780 in Charles City County.

1830

Virginia's population exceeded 1,220,000, but its rank among the United States fell to third place.

In January, at a convention held in Richmond, the Commonwealth adopted its second constitution, which, among other things, more equalized the western counties' representation in the Assembly.

1831

The Virginia Historical Society, the oldest such organization in the South, was founded in Richmond.

Floyd County was created from Montgomery County. Page County was created from parts of Rockingham and Shenandoah Counties.

In a short-lived revolt in August, Nat Turner, a slave from Southampton County, and his followers killed about sixty whites in the region. The rebellion was squashed two days later and Turner was arrested, tried, convicted, and hanged. Thirty slaves were prosecuted while the General Assembly quickly passed more oppressive slave laws.

Cyrus McCormack, a native of Rockbridge County, invented the reaper.

1832

Smyth County was created from parts of Washington and Wythe Counties.

The remaining part of the old Capitol in Williamsburg was destroyed by fire. "I am happy, however, to be able to add that all the Record Books and Papers are saved," wrote A. P. Upshur to Governor John Floyd at Richmond.

The James River and Kanawha Company was chartered by the General Assembly with authorization to raise five million dollars to be used in canal construction.

1833

Rappahannock County (the second county with that name) was created from Culpeper County.

James Ewell Brown (Jeb) Stuart, the "Cavalier of Dixie" – West Point graduate, son-in-law of Union General Philip St. George Cooke, and commander of all cavalry in the Army of Northern Virginia – was born in Patrick County. He was killed in action at Yellow Tavern in May, 1864.

The great jurist, John Marshall, lived in this house in Richmond. A native-born Virginian, he served during the Revolution as one of the Culpeper Minute Men. He was in his thirty-fifth year as chief justice of the United States Supreme Court when he died in Philadelphia in July, 1835.

From old engravings in the author's collection.

1834

The *Southern Literary Messenger*, a popular monthly magazine of the times, was founded in Richmond. Its most famous editor was the renowned poet, Edgar Allan Poe, a graduate of the University of Virginia.

1835

David Bullock, a resident of Richmond, sold Jamestown Island to Goodrich Durfey, who had only recently built a toll-bridge linking the island to the mainland. During the decade of Durfey's ownership, he improved the land to "a high state of . . . cultivation," and boasted that it possessed "the best wheat soil in the state."

1836

Clarke County was created from Frederick County. Warren County was created from parts of Shenandoah and Frederick Counties.

Sam Houston, born near Lexington and a former U. S. congressman from Tennessee and governor of that state, became the president of the Republic of Texas.

1837

Ellen Herndon, wife of Chester Arthur, twenty-first president of the United States, was born in Fredericksburg.

This earliest known view of Alexandria depicts slave ships along the 1830s waterfront.

From a broadside entitled, *The Slave Market in America*,
published by the American Anti-Slavery Society. New York, 1836.

1838

Greene County was created from Orange County.

William Clark, who with Meriwether Lewis in 1804-06 explored the trans-Mississippi River West for President Thomas Jefferson, died in St. Louis, where he had served many years as Indian agent, governor of the Missouri Territory, and Superintendent of Indian Affairs. At the time his funeral procession was the largest public gathering ever recorded in St. Louis to date.

Roanoke County was created from Botetourt County.

1839

Pulaski County was created from parts of Montgomery and Wythe Counties.

Virginia Military Institute (VMI), sometimes called "the West Point of the South," was established. Faculty members over the years have included such noted Virginians as Matthew Fontaine Maury and Thomas J. "Stonewall" Jackson. George Catlett Marshall – United States Army chief of staff, U. S. secretary of state, author of the European Recovery Act, U. S. secretary of defense, and Nobel Peace Prize laureate – graduated from VMI. General George Patton of World War II fame attended there for one year before transferring to West Point.

An 1840s view of the harbors at Norfolk and Portsmouth, as seen from Fort Norfolk.

From *Historical Collections of Virginia,* by Henry Howe. Charleston, South Carolina, 1845.

1840

Virginia's standing among other states in population fell to fourth place with a figure of 1,249,764.

The northern section of the Shenandoah Turnpike was completed linking the towns of Winchester and Staunton. The act authorizing the construction of the macadam-surfaced road was passed by the General Assembly in 1834.

1841

In April, after serving as president of the United States for only one month, William Henry Harrison, the hero of the Battle of Tippecanoe in 1811, died of pneumonia. He was succeeded by the new vice-president, John Tyler. Ironically, both Harrison and Tyler were born in Charles City County.

The invention of the reaper by Rockbridge County native, Cyrus McCormack, was a boon to American farmers everywhere. With the new implement and later improvements upon it, difficult, back-breaking work that had previously taken days could be accomplished in mere hours.

From *Harper's Weekly,* August 1, 1857.

1842

Carroll County was created from Grayson County.

1843

Construction on St. Paul's Episcopal Church in Richmond was begun. Designed in the Greek Revival style, the church's plans were developed by Thomas S. Steward of Philadelphia. Many Virginia notables have worshipped at the church, among them Robert E. Lee, Confederate President Jefferson Davis, and Matthew Fontaine Maury.

A little-known portrait of Edgar Allan Poe.

From a watercolor attributed to J. C. McDougall.

1844

Henrietta Hall, the first American woman to serve as a missionary in China, died in Hong Kong. Born in Lancaster County in 1817, Hall was married to J. Lewis Shuck, a Baptist minister. The couple's Chinese assignment began in 1836.

1845

Appomattox County was created from parts of Buckingham, Prince Edward, Charlotte, and Campbell Counties.

1846

Arlington County (originally called Alexandria County) was created from a section of Fairfax County that had been gifted to the United States government in 1789 but returned during this year. The name was changed to Arlington County in 1920.

Army veterans Winfield Scott and Zachary Taylor, both Virginia-born, assumed high-ranking commands at the outbreak of the Mexican War.

1847

Highland County was created from parts of Pendleton (in present-day West Virginia) and Bath Counties.

Charles Bent, the recently appointed governor of New Mexico Territory, was savagely murdered in Taos during a short-lived rebellion following the occupation of Santa Fe the previous year by the American army. Bent was born in Charleston (in present-day West Virginia) in 1799 and with his brother, William, emigrated west where they established a fur-trading empire on the southern Great Plains.

1848

Joseph Reid Anderson purchased the eleven-year-old Tredegar Iron Works situated on the James River in Richmond. The giant industrial complex played a key role during the War Between the States as it furnished much-needed war materiel to the Confederacy.

An 1840s view of High Street in Richmond.

From an old engraving in the author's collection.

1849

Richmond's Hollywood Cemetery was dedicated. Among the noted people buried there are Matthew Fontaine Maury, John Tyler, James Monroe, and Jefferson Davis.

1850

Virginia retained its fourth place position in population as its figure grew to nearly 1,500,000 people.

By mid-century, railroads in Virginia were rapidly competing with canals and stage lines as a popular mode of transportation.

1851

Craig County was created from parts of Botetourt, Roanoke, Giles, and Monroe (in present-day West Virginia) Counties.

The James River and Kanawha Canal, connecting the towns of Richmond and Buchanan, was completed at a cost of more than eight million dollars.

Walter Reed, the U. S. army physician who discovered the connection between mosquitoes and yellow fever, was born in Gloucester County.

Virginia's third constitution, which guaranteed white, adult males the right to vote and which established the popular vote as the method for electing the governor, was approved at a convention held in Richmond.

1852

Lynchburg, founded in 1786 and named after John Lynch, who owned the original town site, was incorporated as a city.

1853

Thomas Nelson Page, scion of two old Virginia families, was born. Educated at Washington College and the University of Virginia, Page is best known for his book, *In Old Virginia,* published in 1887.

1854

As part of the Compromise of 1850, the Fugitive Slave Bill was voted into law. The act demanded that any slave who fled his or her bondage be immediately returned to the owner. In June, Boston authorities sent Anthony Burns, a young runaway slave back to his Virginia owner. The incident caused a national uproar as women's suffrage and abolitionist groups vigorously protested. In the end, the national government spent more than $100,000 to return Burns to Virginia.

1855

The Hospital of St. Vincent DePaul in Norfolk was founded. It was the town's first civilian hospital and was originally operated out of the home of one of its organizers, Ann Plume Herron.

1856

Wise County was created from parts of Lee, Scott, and Russell Counties.

Woodrow Wilson, twenty-eighth president of the United States, was born in Staunton.

Booker T. Washington, the acclaimed educator and founder of Tuskegee Institute, was born a slave on the James Burroughs plantation in Franklin County.

1857

Citizens of Norfolk, Williamsburg, and the surrounding area celebrated the 250th anniversary of Virginia's first permanent English-speaking settlement.

1858

Buchanan County was created from parts of Tazewell and Russell Counties.

1859

During the morning of February 8, the main building on the campus of the College of William and Mary was engulfed in flames, resulting in a great deal of damage. "The Philosophical and Chemical Apparatus was entirely destroyed, not a single Book was saved from the Library, the Smoke being too dense to enter," reported one observer. Later in the year, Raleigh Tavern also succumbed to flames, resulting in a loss of about fifteen thousand dollars.

In October, John Brown, an abolitionist from Kansas, raided the Federal Armory in Harper's Ferry (present-day West Virginia) with the intention of arming blacks and beginning a rebellion. Within hours, Colonel Robert E.

After the disastrous fire of 1859, the campus at the College of William and Mary took on much of its present-day look.

From *Historical Collections of Virginia,* by Henry Howe. Charleston, South Carolina, 1845.

Following John Brown's abortive raid on Harpers Ferry in October, 1859, the Kansas abolitionist was tried, found guilty of murder and conspiracy, and hanged.

From an old engraving in the author's collection.

Lee and Lieutenant J. E. B. Stuart along with their men captured Brown and his followers and placed them under arrest. A month and a half later, Brown was hanged on charges of murder, treason, and conspiracy.

1860

Virginia's population reached 1,596,318, with approximately one-third of the figure being slaves. The Commonwealth's place in population among other states fell to fifth.

George Washington's home, Mount Vernon, began its life as a national shrine. The house and more than two hundred acres had been purchased the previous year by the Mount Vernon Ladies' Association.

1861

Bland County was created from parts of Giles, Wythe, and Tazewell Counties.

In April, after refusing fellow Virginian and Union General Winfield Scott's offer to command United States troops in what appeared to be a rapidly approaching war, Colonel Robert E. Lee was appointed commander of Virginia troops for the Confederacy.

In May, Virginia became the eighth state to secede from the Union, following the firing on Fort Sumter and President Abraham Lincoln's request for volunteers to suppress the South's defiance. Richmond was named the capital for the newly organized Confederate States of America.

In the first major conflict of the War Between the States, the largest army ever assembled in North America to date met defeat in July at Bull Run Creek in northern Virginia. There, a

Although the majority of Virginians favored secession from the United States in 1861, those who lived in the western, mountainous sections of the Commonwealth were primarily pro-Union. The character of the mountaineer who predominantly lived on small, family-run farms differed greatly from the large-scale plantation owner of the east, who often owned slaves to maintain his holdings.

From *Historical Collections of Virginia,* by Henry Howe. Charleston, South Carolina, 1845.

poorly trained Union force of about thirty-five thousand men and forty-nine guns battled the twenty-two thousand, equally ill-trained, Confederate army poised nearby.

Virginia residents were mixed in their opinions about secession. Those in the Tidewater and Piedmont regions favored separation from the United States, while those in the mountainous west (that part that eventually became West Virginia) cast their lot with the Union. Therefore, from 1861 until the War's end in 1865, two separate state governments functioned in Virginia. At Richmond, Confederate officials were in control under the direction of Governors John Letcher of Rockbridge County (1860-64) and William Smith of Fauquier County (1864-65). Meanwhile, the federally-recognized state government operated from Wheeling, and later, Alexandria, with Francis Harrison Pierpont of Marion County (in today's West Virginia) as governor.

The convention held in Wheeling in June, 1861, laid plans for the admission of the western part of Virginia to be admitted to the Union as a separate state called West Virginia.

From *Harper's Weekly,* issue of July 6, 1861.

In anticipation of rapidly approaching war, Union volunteers at Arlington constructed earthworks around Washington, D. C.

From *Harper's Weekly,* June 15, 1861.

1862

On March 9, the ironclad vessels, *U. S. S. Monitor* and the *C. S. S. Merrimac* (formerly known as the *Virginia*), exchanged vicious fire just off Cape Henry at the entrance to Hampton Roads. The *Monitor* eventually retreated, but neither boat had pierced the other's protecting metal shell.

Union troops occupied Williamsburg in May.

In late May, Robert E. Lee replaced General Joseph E. Johnston as commander of the Army of Northern Virginia. Almost immediately Lee's forces met those of Union General George B. McClellan in a series of skirmishes fought east of Richmond and collectively called the Seven Days Battles. When the combat ended on July 1, the two conflicting armies had suffered nearly forty thousand casualties between them. Although Union forces emerged victorious, they also evacuated the area leaving the city of Richmond temporarily unthreatened.

The naval battle between the U. S. S. Monitor *and the* C. S. S. Merrimac *occurred in March, 1862, at the entrance to Hampton Roads.*

From an old engraving in the author's collection.

Richmond citizens celebrated in front of the Capitol as news of the Confederate victory at Bull Run Creek was announced. The carnival atmosphere surrounding this first major battle of the War Between the States went a long way in giving a sense of false security to officials of the infant Confederate States of America.

From *Frank Leslie's Illustrated Newspaper,* October 6, 1861.

In August, Lee met Union General John Pope in the fields lying along Bull Run Creek for a second major battle in that location. The Army of Northern Virginia routed Pope's forces, who fled across the Potomac River to Maryland, where they prepared themselves for the upcoming battle known as Antietam.

For three days in December, the armies of General Lee and Union General Ambrose E. Burnside, General McClellan's replacement, skirmished at Fredericksburg. The battle was the first of four conflicts that were fought in the neighborhood of the small town on the Rappahannock River. Lee and the Confederates, although outnumbered three to two, claimed the victory after sustaining 5,300 casualties.

1863

The soldiers, Northern and Southern, who fought so tenaciously in combat were not the only people suffering as the second year of the bloody war was ending. In Richmond, during early April, poor and hungry civilians – many of them sick from smallpox and scarlet fever and all of them tired of paying three hundred dollars for a barrel of flour – vented their anger in what became known as the Richmond Bread Riot.

In an early example of federal government support for public housing and assistance, this Freedman's Village atop Greene Heights in Arlington opened in 1863 to provide basic needs for recently freed slaves. In April, 1862, the number of freedmen in the area numbered four hundred. By 1865, the figure had jumped to forty thousand.

Drawing by A. R. Waud. From *Harper's Weekly.*

Still in the Fredericksburg vicinity, the two enemy armies clashed again in late April at Chancellorsville. General Joseph Hooker now led the Union forces which he pitted against Lee's Army of Northern Virginia. When the fighting was over nine days later, Lee had scored an overwhelming victory, but one that was strategically of little importance. He also lost one of his most brilliant lieutenants, General Thomas J. (Stonewall) Jackson, who died of pneumonia after being mistakenly wounded by a Confederate soldier. Lee's victory at Chancellorsville set the stage for his army's invasion of Pennsylvania, where, two months later, it was overpowered at Gettysburg.

The U. S. Congress admitted the western portion of Virginia, that part of the Commonwealth whose voters had elected not to secede from the Union, into the United States as a separate and distinct state to be called West Virginia.

1864

Following its defeat at Gettysburg, the Army of Northern Virginia spent winter quarters (1863-64) near Fredericksburg. In May, the Wilderness Campaign opened fifteen miles west of the town where Union General Ulysses S. Grant (who had succeeded General George G. Meade, who had in turn followed General Joseph Hooker as the commander of the Union army) clashed head-on with General Lee. Casualties for the two-day bloody conflict totaled twenty-five thousand men for both armies. The battle purchased Grant the time he needed to move his army toward Spotsylvania and closer to Richmond, which he wanted to occupy in order to bring a quicker end to the tiring war.

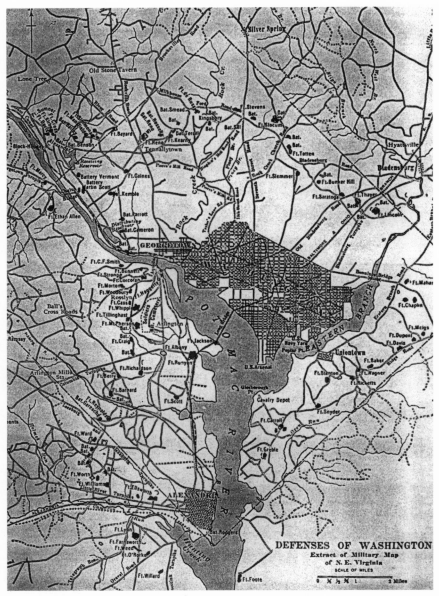

A map of the Federal defense network around Washington, D. C. depicts many forts and other government installations in outlying northern Virginia.

Courtesy of the U. S. National Park Service.

The Battle of Cedar Creek on October 19, 1864, was the last major conflict fought in the Shenandoah Valley. In the fight, General Jubal Early's command suffered considerably at the hands of General Philip Sheridan.

Painting by Carl Rakeman, courtesy of the U. S. Federal Highway Commission.

During the next two weeks, residents in the village of Spotsylvania Court House witnessed the two opposing armies – now totaling around 175,000 men between them – skirmishing with each other to the north and west of town. By the end of the campaign, it was obvious from Grant's move to the south toward Richmond that the future was precarious for the Confederacy.

In short order, Grant laid siege to both Richmond and Petersburg. For the next year, the armies faced one another in a disquieting game of wits. As railroad lines feeding the two cities' commerce were secured by Grant's soldiers, the citizenry quickly began to suffer from the effects of food shortages. By the end of the year, no relief was in sight, and residents could look forward to nothing more than a cold, miserable winter.

Major General James Ewell Brown (Jeb) Stuart – native of Patrick County and the commander of cavalry for the Army of Northern Virginia – died in mid-May of a wound received at Yellow Tavern during the defense of Richmond.

Also in May, in the Shenandoah Valley, Union and Confederate armies clashed at New Market. The boys and young men of the nearby Virginia Military Institute were activated for the battle and performed admirably, resulting in the Union army's retreat up the valley.

1865

The end for the Confederate defenders of the Richmond area came on April 2. General Lee quickly retreated from Petersburg and notified President Jefferson Davis in Richmond to flee the capital. During the night, a crazed mob torched the city and destroyed much war materiel. The conflagration was followed by the entry of General Grant's advancing army. Danville was named the new capital of the Confederacy.

Lee's plan to continue the war by merging his tattered Army of Northern Virginia with the fleeing defenders of Richmond never materialized. After losing nine thousand more men at Sailor's Creek on April 6, Lee found himself near the hamlet of Appomattox Court House with no place to go. "There is nothing left for me to do but to go and see General Grant and I would rather die a thousand deaths," lamented the broken Lee. The staffs of the two generals met in the McLean House in the heart of the village on April 9 and signed the papers ending the war almost four years to the day after the conflict had started.

Within days after the surrender, United States President Abraham Lincoln was assassinated at Ford's Theater in Washington, D. C. His accused killer,

Richmond was set ablaze during the night of April 2 and the early morning hours of April 3, 1865. On the morning of the second, General Robert E. Lee in Petersburg wired President Jefferson Davis in Richmond that "I think it is absolutely necessary that we should abandon our position tonight." By the time the Confederate Government had closed down and officials had evacuated Richmond, unruly mobs had burned the city.

From an old engraving in the author's collection.

Richmond as it appeared when the sun came up on April 3, 1865.

From an old engraving in the author's collection.

an actor by the name of John Wilkes Booth, fled the crime scene immediately. Twelve days later, when U. S. soldiers cornered him in a barn near Port Royal in Caroline County, they set the building ablaze and killed Booth when he attempted to escape the flames.

After fleeing Richmond, Confederate President Jefferson Davis was soon captured in rural Georgia. He was sent back to Virginia where he was indicted for treason and held prisoner at Fort Monroe for two years without a trial.

President Andrew Johnson, Abraham Lincoln's successor, appointed Francis H. Pierpont, as the Commonwealth's provisional governor with headquarters in Richmond. Pierpont, the former West Virginian who had always been recognized by Federal authorities as the Commonwealth's legitimate chief official, took over his duties in May.

1866

Using an elaborate system of kites, Dr. Mahlon Loomis, a local dentist, sent a signal fourteen miles across the mountains of Clarke County in an early experimentation of wireless telegraphy.

The U. S. Congress passed the Fourteenth Amendment to the Constitution. Several features of the amendment were directed toward the states of the former Confederacy. Among other things, they sought to prohibit all former Confederate officials from holding public office and guaranteed all rights to freed slaves. Virginia, along with other Southern states, refused to ratify the amendment.

During Reconstruction, St. Philip's Church in Richmond was converted into a school for former slave children.

From *Harper's Weekly,* May 25, 1867.

1867

Chagrined by the refusal of Southern leaders to ratify the fourteenth amendment, U. S. Congressional leaders enacted the Radical Reconstruction Acts which placed the entire South under the control of the United States Army. Virginia was defined as Military District Number One and was commanded by General John M. Schofield.

1868

General Samuel Chapman Armstrong established Hampton Normal and Agricultural Institute, primarily for freed slaves, in Hampton. Noted educator Booker T. Washington graduated from the facility which was renamed Hampton University in 1984.

James Jeter Phillips, a twenty-four-year-old Henrico County socialite, was executed for murdering his wife and dumping her body into a ditch on his estate.

1869

During the height of Reconstruction, Virginia's fourth constitution, sometimes called the Underwood Constitution after the presiding officer of the convention that approved it, was ratified. The document established a Commonwealth-wide public school system, provided for magisterial districts within each county, and gave all men the right to vote.

1870

Virginia's population among the states of the Union fell to tenth place as the figures plummeted to 1,225,000, nearly the same number as forty years earlier.

In January, by authority of President Ulysses S. Grant, Virginia was readmitted to the United States.

1871

The General Assembly passed the Funding Act of 1871. The highly controversial measure sought to eliminate a large portion of the Commonwealth's debt. Instead, by succumbing to high interest rates to pay off the debt, the act, called "the most disastrous piece of economic legislation in Virginia history," caused a great deal of financial havoc.

1872

Edith Bolling, President Woodrow Wilson's second wife, was born in Wytheville.

Following his illustrious military career, Robert E. Lee was appointed president of Washington College in Lexington (later named Washington and Lee University). He died there on October 12, 1870.

From *The Photographic History of the Civil War,* Robert S. Lanier, editor. New York, 1911.

Virginia Agricultural and Mechanical College, today known as Virginia Polytechnic Institute and State University (Virginia Tech) was established in Blacksburg.

1873

Ilene Langhorne, who became the model for the world famous "Gibson Girl," was born in Danville. Ilene married Charles Dana Gibson in 1895, and shortly afterwards, her artist husband capitalized on her incredible beauty to launch his "girl in the gay '90s" concept.

1874

James William Marshall was appointed U. S. postmaster general by President U. S. Grant. He served in the position for only forty-seven days and was the only Virginian ever to hold the post.

Reedville, a small hamlet in Northumberland County, was founded by Elijah W. Reed, who built a factory at the location to process menhaden. Business was so good that the village soon became the center for the menhaden industry in America.

1875

George Pickett, always remembered for "Pickett's Charge" against the Federal line during the third day at the Battle of Gettysburg, died in Norfolk. Born in Richmond in 1825, Pickett graduated from West Point last in his class of fifty-nine. Following the disastrous charge and despite his own personal bravery, his military reputation suffered greatly.

1876

Richmond became one of the nation's largest producers of cigarettes.

1877

The *Richmond Inquirer,* founded in 1804 by Thomas Richie and one of the Commonwealth's most notable newspapers, ceased publication. In the meantime, Richie had gone on to serve as editor of the *Washington Union.* He died in 1854.

1878

James A. Bland, a former slave, copyrighted his song, *Carry Me Back to Old Virginny.* He had composed the song three years earlier. Years later, the General Assembly adopted Bland's composition as the official state song.

1879

The town of Fredericksburg, founded in 1728 and named in honor of the eldest son of King George II, was bestowed "city" status.

Booker T. Washington was Hampton Institute's most famous student. The son of slaves graduated in 1875 at the head of his class, and, six years later, he organized the Tuskegee Institute in Tuskegee, Alabama. A noted speaker, Washington was a champion for cooperation between blacks and whites and for equality for his people.

From an early photograph.

1880

Virginia's population, now fourteenth in the Nation at just over 1,500,000, numbered less than it did during pre-War Between the States years.

Dickenson County was created from parts of Russell, Wise, and Buchanan Counties.

1881

On July 4, Virginian Booker T. Washington opened the Tuskegee Normal School in Alabama as an institution for black students. He became the facility's first principal.

1882

The town of Big Lick, organized in 1852, was renamed Roanoke.

The dream of Alfred W. Harris, a black Dinwiddie County attrney and a member of the House of Delegates, was fulfilled when Virginia State University (originally called Virginia Normal and Collegiate Institute) was organized. The school, located in Ettrick, near Petersburg, became the nation's first state-sponsored, four-year accredited university dedicated to higher learning for black students.

1883

Ten-year-old Willa Cather, who won the Pulitzer Prize for her 1927 novel, *Death Comes for the Archbishop,* left her home in Frederick County wih her family for new beginnings in Nebraska.

The Norfolk and Western Railroad laid a line from Radford to the newly discovered coal fields along the Virginia-West Virgia border, allowing coal to ship directly to the Atlantic coast for export.

1884

The State Female Normal School opened in Farmville. In 1914, it changed its name to State Normal School for Women at Farmville. Ten years later, its name changed again, this time to State Teachers' College at Farmville.

1885

In early June, fire destroyed the lunatic hospital at Williamsburg, killing one patient, displacing 224 others, and causing serious damage to several buildings.

1886

Douglas Southall Freeman – editor, historian, prolific author, and Pulitzer Prize-winning biographer of George Washington and Robert E. Lee – was born in Lynchburg.

1887

Brothers Paul D., James L., and Robert J. Camp – sawmill operators in Isle of Wight County – organized the Camp Manufacturing Company which later became the industrial giant, Union Camp Corporation. The company was a pioneer in reforestation efforts on lands that had been cleared of marketable timber.

1888

The world's first electric railway system was implemented in Richmond. Called the Richmond Union Passenger Railway, the system consisted of forty cars running on twelve miles of track. Designed by Frank Julian Sprague, the railway operated until 1949.

1889

The Association for the Preservation of Virginia Antiquities (APVA) was organized.

1890

Virginia's population, now fifteenth in the Nation, approached 1,700,000.

John Mercer Langston (1829-1897), a former slave from Petersburg, became Virginia's first elected black member of the U. S. House of Representatives.

1891

Randolph-Macon Woman's College was founded in Lynchburg. It was the first women's college to be admitted to the Southern Association of Colleges and Secondary Schools. Among its alumni was Pearl Buck, novelist and first American woman to win the Nobel Prize for Literature.

1892

Joseph Reid Anderson died. Born in Botetourt County in 1813 Anderson was the master of the giant Tredegar Iron Works in Richmond, the firm that produced a prodigious quantity of war materiel for the Confederacy. A West Point graduate, he later served as a brigade commander under General A. P. Hill during the Seven Days' campaigns.

1893

In May, the Association for the Preservation of Virginia Antiquities acquired nearly twenty-three acres on Jamestown Island, which, when added to the property conveyed to them the previous year by the General Assembly, set the stage for the Association's thrust to perpetuate the story of Jamestown's colonization in 1607.

1894

The village of Washington, located in Rappahannock County, was incorporated. According to most authorities, the town's site was surveyed by George Washington in 1749 and was the first community in the United States to bear the name of the first president.

The Pulaski county seat was moved from Newburn to Pulaski.

1895

Matthew Bunker Ridgway was born at Fortress Monroe, son of an artillery colonel. Ridgway went on to become a West Point graduate; veteran of service in Nicaragua, Panama, and the Philippines; commander of the U. S. 82nd Airborne Division and XVIII Corps in World War II; commander of United Nations forces during the Korean War; NATO commander; and U. S. army chief of staff.

1896

William Munford Tuck – World War I veteran, attorney, Virginia delegate, Virginia senator, lieutenant-governor, governor, and U. S. congressman – was born in Halifax County.

1897

Saint Emma's Industrial and Agricultural School opened in Belmead, the former home of Philip St. George Cooke located in Powhatan County. The Gothic Revival home was designed by noted architect, Alexander Jackson Davis, and built in 1845. Saint Emma's was operated by the Catholic Church until the 1970s for the benefit of black students.

1898

American Consul-General Fitzhugh Lee, born in 1835 in Fairfax County and the nephew of Robert E. Lee, had served in Cuba for two years, when January street riots in Havana prompted him to wire the U. S. Navy for a ship to be dispatched as a show of strength. He soon retracted his request, but by then the *U. S. S. Maine* was already on its way, docking in the harbor later in the month. Two weeks later, the *Maine* was destroyed by an explosion of unknown origin.

1899

Americans everywhere observed the one-hundredth anniversary of President George Washington's death.

1900

Population figures for Virginia revealed that the Commonwealth had fallen to seventeenth place in the Nation with 1,854,184 residents.

1901

In an effort to provide better medical care for poor families in Richmond, a group of dedicated churchwomen organized the Instructive Visiting Nurses' Association.

George Catlett Marshall – U. S. army chief of staff, U. S. secretary of both the state and the defense departments, author of Europe's postwar recovery program, and Nobel Peace Prize laureate – graduated from Virginia Military Institute with a first captain's rank.

1902

The Commonwealth's fifth constitution was adopted by a convention called in Richmond in June, 1901. It became effective on July 10, 1902 and was unique in that its ratification was proclaimed by the convention, rather than becoming valid upon a popular vote. Among other changes, the new instrument established a poll tax as a qualifier for voting.

1903

One of Virginia's worst tragedies occurred in Danville in late September when a Southern Railroad train veered off a trestle and plummeted to the gulch far below, killing nine people. The accident inspired the popular song of the day, "The Wreck of the Old 97."

Anne Bannister Spencer, a leading spirit in the genre of writing called Harlem Renaissance, moved to Lynchburg where she lived until her death in 1975. It was while living there that a large body of her poems was published between the years 1920 and 1935.

1904

Maggie L. Walker (1867-1934), the first woman in the United States to become president of a bank, purchased her home in Richmond. Walker, the CEO of the Saint Luke Penny Savings Bank, was also a founder of the Richmond Council of Colored Women. Today, the house is a National Historic Landmark.

The wreck of the old '97 occurred in 1903 when a mail train veered off the tracks in downtown Danville.

From an old engraving in the author's collection.

1905

Joseph Cotten, Hollywood heartthrob of the 1930s, 40s, and 50s, was born in Petersburg. Cotton played in a number of movies including *The Third Man* with Orson Wells. He died in 1994.

1906

John Baptist Pierce became the first black farm demonstration agent for the Commonwealth. For the rest of his life, Pierce served in various agricultural occupations in both Virginia and North Carolina and as a U. S. Department of Agriculture field agent.

1907

President Theodore Roosevelt attended the 300th anniversary of the founding of Jamestown. The gala festivities were held at Norfolk and lasted from April 26 until November 30. One of the highlights of the occasion was when Roosevelt launched part of the United States Atlantic Fleet on its maiden voyage around the world. Several of the buildings erected especially for the celebration later became part of the Norfolk Naval Base. On Jamestown Island itself, the old church was rebuilt and the John Smith and Pocahontas statues were dedicated.

1908

Staunton became the first city in the nation to adopt the city manager form of local government.

1909

The Equal Suffrage League was organized in Richmond by Ellen Glasgow, Mary Johnston, Adele Clark, Lila Meade Valentine, and Kate Langley Bosher. It soon became a leading voice in Virginia's fight for women's voting rights. Although by 1920, the Nineteenth Amendment allowing women the right to vote had become the law of the land, the Virginia General Assembly refused to ratify the measure until 1952.

1910

Virginia's population reached 2,061,612.

In November, modern naval aviation was born when Eugene Ely flew a Curtiss "Hudson Flyer" from the deck of the *U. S. S. Birmingham*, moored about three miles offshore from Fort Monroe, to a landing strip at Willoughby Spit.

On April 26, 1907, President Theodore Roosevelt addressed several thousand guests assembled for the gala 300ᵗʰ anniversary celebration of Jamestown's founding, telling them that "the fact that so many of our people, of whom as it happens I myself am one, have but a very small portion of English blood in our veins, in no way alters the fact that this nation was founded by Englishmen." The affair was held at Sewell's Point in Norfolk and was funded by a $200,000 appropriation from the General Assembly.

Photograph from *Leslie's Illustrated Weekly*,
September 18, 1902.

1911

A state-operated colony for the treatment of epileptic and mentally-challenged patients opened near Lynchburg.

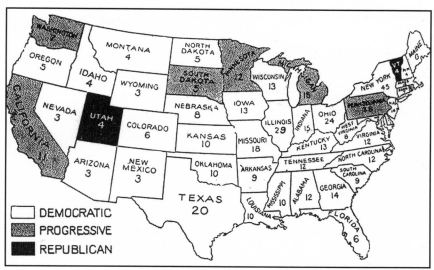

Staunton native and Democratic Party presidential nominee Woodrow Wilson easily won the electoral vote of 1912 as shown on this national map. Only Vermont and Utah voted Republican, while several other states cast their votes for the Progressive Party's candidate, former President Theodore Roosevelt.

Map from *American Monthly Review of Reviews*, December, 1912.

1912

On the forty-sixth ballot cast at the Democratic National Convention in Baltimore, Staunton-born Woodrow Wilson was nominated as the party's presidential nominee. Although he won the electoral college with a vote of 435 to incumbent President William Howard Taft's eight, Wilson tallied only forty-two per cent of the popular vote in the fall elections.

1913

The State Normal and Industrial School for Women opened in Radford. In 1924 the name was changed to Radford State Teachers College. Becoming a division of Virginia Polytechnic Institute in 1944, it was renamed again to Radford College. The school became co-educational in 1972 and achieved university status in 1979.

1914

The Farm Demonstration Agency was transferred to the control of Virginia Polytechnic Institute and became known as the Agricultural Extension Service.

Residents in rural Virginia received a welcome addition to their mail service in 1913, when parcel post was added to the amenities of the Rural Free Delivery (RFD) system. RFD was begun in 1896, but heretofore included only letter delivery.

Painting by Carl Rakeman, courtesy of the Federal Highway Administration.

1915

Carter Godwin Woodson, one of the first blacks in America to earn a Ph. D. from Harvard University, organized the Association for the Study of Negro Life and History. Born in 1875 in Buckingham County, Woodson also was the founder of the *Journal of Negro History.* He died in 1950 in Washington, D. C.

The first trans-Atlantic radio-telephone communication was transmitted between Arlington and Paris, France.

Rosewell, one of Virginia's most beautiful plantation houses was destroyed by fire in March, 1916. This photograph shows the mansion as it appeared just prior to the blaze.

Photograph by H. P. Cook.

1916

On a windy March day, the manor house at Rosewell Plantation, situated on a spit of land jutting into the York River, burned, leaving only the four walls as silent reminders of its past glory. Built on land originally granted in 1639 to George Menefie, the house was completed by Mathew Page near the end of the seventeenth century.

1917

From June until December, a large number of women suffragettes, arrested by Washington, D. C. police for picketing the White House, were imprisoned in a workhouse in Fairfax County.

General Samuel D. Rockenbach, born in Lynchburg in 1869, was appointed the first chief of the U. S. Army Tank Corps. His pioneering efforts with the newly introduced tank helped pave the way for the army to rapidly attain superiority with the weapon and were directly responsible for its success on the European battlefields during World War I. For his contributions, Rockenbach is called the "father" of United States Army tank warfare.

1918

By this pivotal year in World War I, shipyards in Hampton Roads had produced more naval-craft tonnage than the combined efforts of all other manufacturers in America.

In order to "foster a feeling of pride in our State and stimulate an interest in the history and traditions of the Commonwealth," the General Assembly adopted a resolution making the American dogwood (*Cornus florida*) the state flower.

General Samuel D. Rockenbach, born in Lynchburg in 1869, was appointed the first chief of the U.S. Army Tank Corps. For creating the American tank force that served with great distinction in the last months of World War I, he is remembered as the "father" of U.S. army tank warfare."

Photograph courtesy of the United States Signal Corps.

Virginia shipyards produced hundreds of naval vessels during both the World War I and World War II years.

Photograph courtesy of the United States Signal Corps.

1919

Studies were performed at the Experimental Farm of the Bureau of Public Roads in Arlington to measure the destructive impact of gasoline-driven trucks on the nation's highway system. In the July issue of *Public Roads,* it was reported that, indeed, the solid rubber tires of large trucks were largely responsible for the demise of roadways across the country.

President Woodrow Wilson was awarded the Nobel Peace Prize.

1920

Virginia's population topped the 2,300,000 mark.

In August, after years of struggle, Virginia women finally won the right to vote.

1921

The Appalachian Trail is a 2,015-mile footpath that stretches through fourteen states along the crest of the Appalachian Mountains, from Springer

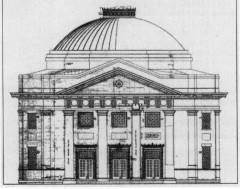

By 1919 Richmond's Beth Ahabah Synagogue was being described as "the handsomest and most commodious synagogue in the South." Formed in 1841 by German Jews, the Beth Ahabah congregation dedicated their building in 1904. It is located on West Franklin Street.

During the late teens and early 1920s, the U. S. Bureau of Public Roads operated a vehicle "experimental farm" on the marshy land situated between Arlington National Cemetery and the Potomac River. There, officials performed all sorts of experiments with automobiles, trucks, and other wheeled vehicles. One such experiment dealt with the impact that the solid rubber tires of large trucks had on various types of pavement. It was determined that, indeed, such hard tires did cause considerable damage to the nation's highway system, designed as it was primarily for horse, buggy, and wagon travel.

Painting by Carl Rakeman.
Painting and map courtesy of the
Federal Highway Administration.

1921 PNEUMATIC TIRE IMPACT TESTS

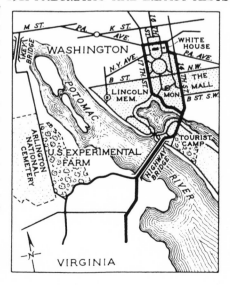

Mountain, Georgia, to Mount Katahdin, Maine. About twenty-five per cent of the Trail's total mileage is contained within Virginia, entering the state in the south near Damascus and exiting in the north several miles beyond Front Royal. The Trail dates to this year when Benton MacKaye sat down with two associates and described to them his dream of creating "a trail that would run in a wilderness belt from one of the highest mountains in New England to one of the highest in the South."

Henry D. "Hal" Flood, Appomattox County native and longtime member of the U. S. House of Representatives where he served as chairman of the Committee on Foreign Affairs, died in Washington, D. C.

1922

The Poe Museum, featuring one of the world's largest collections of Edgar Allan Poe memorabilia, opened in the Old Stone House in downtown Richmond.

1923

Montview, the home of Carter Glass, was built in Lynchburg. Glass was the principal author of the act that established the Federal Reserve System. He also served as U. S. secretary of the treasury and in both houses of the U.S. Congress for a total of forty-two years.

1924

In January, Virginia voters selected Sarah Lee Fain and Helen Timmons Henderson to become the Commonwealth's first female members of the House of Delegates.

1925

Harry Flood Byrd, a Winchester native, was elected Virginia's governor. He quickly and efficiently reorganized the state government and began to build a powerful political base within the Democratic party. In 1933, he was sent to the U. S. Senate where he served until 1965, by which time he had established himself as the predominant figure in Commonwealth politics.

1926

Reverend W. A. R. Goodwin, the rector of Bruton Parish Church in Williamsburg, convinced John D.Rockefeller, Jr. to underwrite the restoration of Virginia's colonial capital city. The first property slated for revival was the Ludwell-Paradise House on Duke of Gloucester Street.

1927

In a crude studio in Bristol, Tennessee, the soon-to-be famous Carter Family of southwestern Virginia – A. P., his wife Sara, and sister-in-law Maybelle – recorded their first musical efforts for Victor Records. Six titles were cut at the session, but it was not until the following year when A. P.'s version of "Wildwood Flower" was released that the group's popularity was assured.

1928

The nation's first Ruritan Club was organized in Holland. Club members seek to better their rural communities through good will and service to their neighbors.

Henry Whitter, an employee of the Fries Textile Plant in Grayson County, traveled to New York City where he recorded his renditions of two mountain tunes, "The Wreck of the Old Southern 97" and "Lonesome Road Blues." This first effort marked an early milestone in the interest in country music and its overwhelming success in the United States.

Martinsville, in Henry County, was made a city by court order. The community, named after Joseph Martin, an early settler, was organized in 1791 and became a town 1873.

1929

Richard Evelyn Byrd, member of the famous family from Winchester, along with three companions, became the first men to fly over the South Pole. Three years earlier Byrd and Floyd Bennett achieved fame as the first to fly over the North Pole. Before he died in 1957, Byrd had made four other trips to the South Pole and in the process added enormously to the scientific data of the most desolate spot on Earth.

At about 8:55 A. M. New York time on Friday, November 29, 1929, Commander Richard E. Byrd wired The New York Times *that "My calculations indicate that we have reached the vicinity of the South Pole, flying high for a survey. The airplane is in good shape, crew all well. Will soon turn north. We can see an almost limitless polar plateau."*

Drawing from *The New York Times,* **November 30, 1929.**

Civil rights activist Vernon Johns began a five-year term of office as the president of Virginia Seminary and College in Lynchburg.

1930
The Commonwealth's population approached 2,500,000.

1931
On January 29, a massive strike among textile workers at a mill in Danville ended. More than four thousand employees had been laid off the previous September. Before affairs were back to normal, Governor John G. Pollard had called in three companies of Virginia national guardsmen.

The old Court House at Williamsburg, in continuous use since before the Revolutionary War, was bequeathed to the Colonial Williamsburg Foundation by officials of the City of Williamsburg and James City County.

1932
The George Washington Grist Mill Historical Park located in Fairfax County was dedicated in celebration of Washington's two hundredth birthday. It was the first such park established in Virginia. Meanwhile, in Alexandria, the George Washington Masonic Memorial was also opened to commemorate the same occasion.

Grand Ole Opry legend Patsy Cline was born in Winchester.

1933
In April, the Civilian Conservation Corps (CCC), one of newly-elected President Franklin D. Roosevelt's "alphabet" agencies designed to help bring the U. S. out of the Great Depression, opened its first camp in the George Washington National Forest in the Blue Ridge Mountains.

The Mount Vernon Memorial Parkway, linking Washington, D. C. with George Washington's home, Mount Vernon, was completed.

Robert Porterfield organized and opened the renowned Barter Theater in Abington.

Richard C. Dupont set a new distance record when he flew his sailplane for nearly 122 miles between Afton Mountain in Nelson County and Frederick, Maryland.

1934
This year marked the perceived completion of the Williamsburg Restoration, begun in 1926. By now, four hundred intrusive buildings had been demolished and 150 period structures had been restored. The Capitol

Building and the Governor's Palace were dedicated, and President Franklin D. Roosevelt attended the formal opening of the Duke of Gloucester Street, calling the thoroughfare "the most historic avenue in America." Actually restoration at Williamsburg is an ongoing and apparently never ending project.

1935

Douglas Southall Freeman was awarded the Pulitzer Prize for his four-volume biography of Robert E. Lee. In 1958, he was posthumously awarded another Pulitzer for the first six volumes of his projected seven-volume biography of George Washington.

1936

Douthat State Park in Alleghany County and Fairy Stone State Park in Patrick County were opened to the public. Both parks were cooperatively developed by the Civilian Conservation Corps (CCC) and the Virginia Conservation Commission.

1937

Labor organizer and United Mines Workers (UMW) President John L. Lewis moved to his new home in Alexandria, located on property once owned by "Light-Horse Harry" Lee. The following year, the former coal miner was named president of the newly organized Congress of Industrial Organizations (CIO).

1938

With assistance from the Works Progress Administration (WPA), work on the Norfolk Botanical Gardens began. Hundreds of unemployed farm workers from the area were hired at wages ranging between twenty-one and seventy-five dollars per month to convert a 120 acre tract of marshland into the dream of City Manager Thomas Thompson.

The historic Chesapeake and Ohio Canal, which in its heyday connected Washington, D. C. with Cumberland, Maryland, was purchased by the United States government for two million dollars. Although it was later threatened by development, the canal and its surrounding area were saved for posterity in 1954 through the efforts of U. S. Supreme Court associate justice William O. Douglas.

Pearl Buck, a 1914 graduate of Randolph-Macon Woman's College, was awarded the Nobel Prize for literature. She had already won the Pulitzer Prize in 1932 for her book *The Good Earth*.

1939

Pittsylvania County native Claude Augustus Swanson — former U. S. congressman, former governor of Virginia, former U. S. senator, and U. S. secretary of the navy during most of President Franklin D. Roosevelt's first two terms died.

1940

Virginia's population approached 2,700,000.

In order to "develop and foster among our citizens and particularly among the children of our schools a feeling of pride in and affection for our Commonwealth," the General Assembly adopted *Carry Me Back to Old Virginia* as the official state song. James A. Bland, a black man, had written the song in 1875 and copyrighted it three years later with the title, *Carry Me Back to Old Virginny."*

Robert Russa Moton, one of the founders of the Urban League and an advisor to five United States presidents, died in Gloucester County. The successor of Booker T. Washington to the presidency of Tuskegee Institute in 1915, Moton was born in Amelia County in 1867 and educated at Hampton Institute.

The Pope-Leighey House in Falls Church, an example of the architectural style of noted American architect Frank Lloyd Wright, was built.

1941

One of the many projects advocated by the government-mandated Federal Writers' Project was a proposed book to be entitled, *America Eats.* It was to provide "a general introduction on development of American cookery" along with individual "sections covering the country by regions." Virginia Writers' Project workers first learned of the proposed book in October, when Eudora Ramsay Richardson notified them and requested that they "submit stories of some typical festivities, emphasizing Virginia foods." The book was never published.

1942

Richmond native Ellen Glasgow was awarded the Pulitzer Prize in literature for her novel, *In This Our Life.*

Camp Pickett, whose name honors Confederate Major General George E. Pickett, was opened on a 46,000- acre tract along the Nottoway River southwest of Petersburg. It served as a training facility for several combat divisions that were later assigned to the European and Pacific theaters during World War II. Now known as Fort Pickett, the post continues its training mission.

1943

U. S. Marines officer Lewis "Chesty" Burwell Puller, born in West Point in 1898, wrote to his military commander, "It is respectfully requested that my present assignment to a combat unit be extended until the downfall of the Japanese government." Puller was called a "Marine's Marine," and he led men in nineteen campaigns from Haiti to Korea, eventually being promoted to lieutenant general in 1955. He died in Hampton in 1971, one of the nation's most highly-decorated soldiers.

1944

Edward Reilly Stettinius, Jr., a native of Illinois but living in Virginia at the time, succeeded Cordell Hull as U. S. secretary of state in President Franklin D. Roosevelt's cabinet. After FDR's death, Stettinius continued his role into President Harry Truman's administration.

1945

By this last year of World War II, some 1,700,000 men and women had processed through the Hampton Roads Port of Embarkation on their way to overseas assignments. Meanwhile, in Newport News, shipyard workers had assembled approximately four hundred ships with a total burden of 3,500,000 tons.

1946

In a landmark case that considered the practice of racial segregation in interstate commerce, the United States Supreme Court ruled in *Morgan vs. Commonwealth of Virginia* that the existing practice was illegal.

1947

United States Secretary of State George C. Marshall introduced his plan for European recovery at Harvard University. Known as the Marshall Plan, it provided money, materiel, and other assistance to a variety of European nations suffering

VMI graduate, George C. Marshall, was the "father" of European Recovery following World War II. During his long and brilliant career, Marshall served as United States Army chief of staff, secretary of state, president of the United States Red Cross, and secretary of defense.

Photograph courtesy of the United States Army.

from the economic hardships of World War II. Although he was born in Pennsylvania, Marshall could trace his ancestry to Virginia; in addition, he had graduated from the Virginia Military Institute in 1901. A week after graduation, he married Elizabeth Carter Coles of Lexington.

1948
Oliver W. Hill, a black attorney from Richmond, was elected to the city council.

1949
Noted biographer Douglas Southall Freeman retired as rector and president of the board of trustees at the University of Richmond.

1950
During the past ten years, Virginia's population surged more than 500,000 to a total of 3,318,680.

The General Assembly passed legislation adopting the Northern Cardinal (*Cardinalis cardinalis*) as the official bird of the Commonwealth because of "its bright plumage and cheerful song."

In 1949, the U. S. Post Office Department issued this stamp to commemorate the two hundredth anniversary of the founding of Washington and Lee University.

Scott Stamp Catalog Number 982.

1951
General Matthew B. Ridgway, born in 1895 at Fortress Monroe where his father served as an artillery officer, replaced General Douglas MacArthur as United Nations commander of Allied forces in Korea. He later served as commander of NATO and U. S. army chief of staff.

1952
Two years before the 1954 *Brown vs. Board of Public Education of Topeka, Kansas* case in which the U. S. Supreme Court declared that segregation in public schools was unconstitutional, a federal district court, in *Davis vs. County School Board of Prince Edward County,* delivered basically the same ruling.

Thirty-two years after the nineteenth amendment to the U. S. Constitution was ratified by a majority of state legislatures thus allowing women the right to vote, Virginia's General Assembly finally passed its own ratification measure.

In April, 1951, Matthew Bunker Ridgway, born in 1895 at Fort Monroe, succeeded another warrior with Virginia ties, General Douglas MacArthur, as supreme Allied commander in Korea. Ridgway also served as chief of staff of the United States Army.

Photograph courtesy of the Harry S. Truman Library.

1953

Thomas Calhoun Walker, the Consultant and Advisor on Negro Affairs in President Franklin D. Roosevelt's Works Progress Administration, died in Gloucester County. Walker was earlier appointed to the post of collector of customs for Virginia by President William McKinley, and he also was a member of Gloucester's board of supervisors. He was the first black man to practice law in Gloucester County.

George C. Marshall was awarded the Nobel Peace Prize.

1954

On July 15, near Glasgow, the temperature reached 110 degrees Fahrenheit, tying the Commonwealth's all-time high record set on July 5, 1900 at Columbia.

The General Assembly passed legislation adopting the official salute to the Commonwealth's flag. It reads, "I salute the flag of Virginia, with reverence and patriotic devotion to the 'Mother of States and Statesmen,' which it represents – the 'Old Dominion,' where liberty and independence were born."

1955

Members of the singing group that eventually became known as the Statler Brothers began their illustrious career at the Lyndhurst Methodist Church in Staunton. Known then as the Kingsmen, original partners were Lew De Witt, Harold Reid, and Phil Balsley. Don Reid, Harold's brother, joined in 1960.

1956

The General Assembly adopted the dogwood *(Cornus florida)* as the Commonwealth's official tree. It had already been designated the state flower in 1918.

1957

Richard E. Byrd, Winchester native and world-renowned Arctic and Antarctic explorer, died in Boston, Massachusetts on March 11.

The Abby Aldrich Rockefeller Folk Art Museum, housing the lifetime collection of Mrs. John D. Rockefeller, Jr., opened in Williamsburg.

Queen Elizabeth II visited Jamestown on the occasion of the 350th anniversary of Jamestown's founding.

Jamestown Festival Park opened to the public.

1958

Virginia Estelle Randolph, named in 1908 as the nation's first Jeanes Supervising Industrial Teacher by the Anna T. Jeanes Fund, died. Randolph, whose parents were slaves, developed an educational system wherein she combined the teaching of conventional subjects with vocational training. The Virginia Randolph Education Center in Henrico County, named in her honor, is the site of her grave.

1959

A movement orchestrated by Senator Harry Byrd and *Richmond News Leader* editor James J. Kilpatrick to defy the 1954 U. S. Supreme Court's decision to desegregate public schools was given a severe blow in January when the Virginia Senate, by a one vote margin, struck down many of the Commonwealth's pro-segregation policies.

1960

Virginia's population approached 4,000,000 residents.

1961

Fairfax, originally called Providence when it was established in 1805, was bestowed city status by court order.

Mrs. Woodrow Wilson, the former Edith Bolling of Wytheville, died in Washington, D. C.

1962

A legislative study commissioned by the General Assembly reported that deepening the James River channel between Richmond and Hampton Roads would do no harm to the river's oyster beds. It also stated that Hampton Roads, "with its vast servicing facilities . . . will benefit" from the procedure.

1963

President John F. Kennedy, stricken down by an assassin's bullet in Dallas, Texas, was buried at Arlington National Cemetery.

1964

The Chesapeake Bay Bridge-Tunnel, connecting Virginia Beach with the Eastern Shore, was opened.

The birth of naval aviation, which occurred offshore from Fort Monroe, was honored by the issue of this commemorative stamp by the United States Post Office in 1961.

Scott Stamp Catalog Number 1185.

Built at a cost of nearly one-half billion dollars, the massive construction project stretches over and under the Bay for a distance of almost eighteen miles.

Nancy Langhorne, the first woman to sit in the British Parliament, died. Born in Danville in 1879, Langhorne began her tenure in the House of Commons in 1919 and served until 1945.

1965

With the election of Mills E. Godwin, Jr. to the governor's chair, the era of Harry Byrd-dominated politics in Virginia came to an end.

1966

Based on the fact that all foxhounds in America are descendants of the original dogs imported by George Washington into Virginia, the General Assembly decreed that the American foxhound be named the official state dog.

The state poll tax was ruled unconstitutional, thus setting the stage for the elimination of poll taxes in all states. The tax had kept several generations of poorer Virginians from the voting booth.

1967

Natural Tunnel State Park was established in Scott County. The 603-acre park features an 850-foot-long tunnel that was naturally carved from the surrounding limestone.

1968

The demise of racial segregation was hastened in Virginia when the U.S. Supreme Court ruled in *Green vs. County School Board of New Kent County* that clear, definable results toward desegregation of the state's public school systems must be demonstrated.

William Styron a native of Newport News was awarded the Pulitzer Prize for his best-selling novel, *The Confessions of Nat Turner.* The book was based on the infamous 1831 slave revolt that occurred in Southampton County.

1969

Warren E. Burger became the first Virginian since John Marshall to hold the position of chief justice of the United States Supreme Court.

Dropping twenty-five inches of rain within a five hour period on August 20, the storms produced by Hurricane *Camille* wracked devastation on much of central Virginia and caused more than $100,000,000 in damages. One thousand bridges and buildings were destroyed. More than one hundred people were killed and thirty-seven were declared missing as the entire Commonwealth was declared a disaster area by the federal government.

1970

Virginia's population reached more than 4,600,000.

Abner Linwood Holton, Jr., a native of Roanoke, was elected the Commonwealth's first Republican governor in one hundred years.

Following the deeding of Carter's Grove Plantation to the Colonial Williamsburg Foundation in 1969, archaeological excavations were begun on the property which resulted, several years later, in the unearthing of Martin's Hundred, the site of an English farm settlement dating back to around 1620.

The Appalachian Trail runs for 549 miles, one-fourth of its total distance, across Virginia. Completed in 1937, the pathway was designated the Appalachian National Scenic Trail in 1968.

Painting by Carl Rakeman. Painting courtesy of the Federal Highway Administration.

1971

The sixth and, so far, the last of the Commonwealth's constitutions was approved by the General Assembly and ratified by voters in November, 1970, to become effective on July 1 of this year. The new instrument provided protection of the environment, as well as guarantees against discrimination by the government based on race, sex, color, or national origin.

Lewis Franklin Powell, Jr. was appointed to the United States Supreme Court by President Richard M. Nixon, his term to become effective on January 7 of the following year.

1972

Tropical Storm *Agnes* spawned a series of devastating floods across the Commonwealth.

1973

The Association for the Preservation of Virginia Antiquities (APVA) purchased the historic structure, Bacon's Castle, briefly used by the Virginia firebrand Nathaniel Bacon during late 1676 when he and his rebel followers burned Jamestown to the ground.

Divers located the ironclad vessel, *U. S. S. Monitor*, off the coast of North Carolina in 220 feet of water. In 1862, the *Monitor* and its Confederate counterpart, the *Merrimack,* had fought each other "mercilessly, but ineffectively" for four hours in Hampton Roads. The boat was lost in a storm on December 30, 1862.

1974

On December 1, a Washington, D. C. - bound jetliner plummeted into the Blue Ridge Mountain wilderness, killing ninety-two passengers.

Michael Learned was awarded the Emmy for best actress in a dramatic role for her performance on *The Waltons,* the immensely popular TV series created and written by Schuyler, Virginia native, Earl Hamner.

1975

Two Virginia writers, Dumas Malone and Anne Dillard, were awarded Pulitzer Prizes. Malone took the prize in history for his multi-volume work, *Jefferson and His Time.* Dillard won her prize in General Nonfiction for *Pilgrim at Tinker Creek.*

Arthur Ashe from Richmond became the first black man to win at Wimbledon.

The Association for the Preservation of Virginia Antiquities (APVA) was responsible for the 1973 purchase and later restoration of Bacon's Castle, one of the Commonwealth's most treasured properties.

From *Frank Leslie's Illustrated Weekly,* September 8, 1866.

1976

The town of Poquoson was bestowed city status by court order.

1977

Bluefield College, opened in 1922 as "an institution of learning for the instruction of boys and men and girls and women in literature, philosophy and the liberal and useful arts," was accredited as a four-year institution.

1978

John Nichols Dalton, Republican from Radford, was inaugurated governor of the Commonwealth.

1979

Eva F. Scott entered the Virginia senate as its first woman member.

Kylene Barker, a twenty-two-year-old beauty from Galax, ruled as "Miss America."

1980

Virginia's population exploded past the five million mark with a total figure of 5,346,818.

In a landmark case for the newspaper industry, the U. S. Supreme Court ruled in *Richmond Newspapers Inc. vs. Virginia* that only during rare situations could news media be excluded from criminal trials.

William Styron was awarded the National Book Award for fiction for *Sophie's Choice*. Richmond author Tom Wolfe won the same prize for nonfiction for his book, *The Right Stuff.*

1981

Jefferson and His Time, a monumental, six-volume work by Dumas Malone about the nation's third president, was completed nearly thirty-three years after it was begun.

1982

In early January, immediately after leaving Washington's National Airport, a jetliner crashed into a bridge spanning the frigid Potomac River killing seventy-one passengers along with seven other people who were crossing the bridge.

1983

William Munford Tuck – U. S. Marine Corps veteran, former member of both houses of Virginia government, former lieutenant-governor and governor, and former U. S. congressman – died in South Boston. Tuck was instrumental in the passage of the Commonwealth's Right to Work legislation.

1984

Norfolk resident Edythe C. Harrison was picked as the Democratic Party nominee for the U. S. Senate, the first woman so honored in Virginia.

1985

A new record low temperature for the Commonwealth – thirty degrees below zero – was set on January 22 at the Mountain Lake Biological Station.

Miles Carpenter, a Sussex County sawmill operator whose wood-carved figures became world-renowned as folk art, died at his home in Waverly.

Williamsburg's Public Hospital, dedicated in 1773 as the first facility for the mentally ill in British North America and destroyed by fire in 1885, was reopened by the Colonial Williamsburg Foundation as an exhibits building featuring the history of the institution and its inmates.

1986

Mary Sue Terry, a resident of Patrick County, became the Commonwealth's first female attorney-general.

1987

Commonwealth voters approved a state-run lottery for the generation of new revenues.

1988

The Chesapeake Bay Deadrise, a small boat featuring a sharp bow and small cabin and used for fishing and oystering, was declared the official state boat by the General Assembly.

1989

Secretariat, thoroughbred racing's Triple Crown winner for 1973, died at the age of nineteen. Born and trained on Meadow Farm in Caroline County, Secretariat holds the record for the fastest time ever run at the Kentucky Derby: 1 minute, 59 2/5 seconds. Riva Ridge, the 1972 Kentucky Derby and Belmont Stakes winner was also born at Meadow Farm.

In 1985, one hundred years after it was destroyed by fire, the Public Hospital reopened in Colonial Williamsburg. Today, the building houses exhibits depicting mental health care during the eighteenth and nineteenth centuries and serves as the entrance to the DeWitt Wallace Decorative Arts Museum.

From an old engraving in the author's collection.

1990

The Commonwealth's population soared to 6,187,358, thereby qualifying it for an additional seat in the U. S. House of Representatives. Approximately seventy-two per cent of Virginia's residents lived in eight urban areas: Northern Virginia; Norfolk, Virginia Beach, and Newport News; Richmond and Petersburg; Roanoke; Lynchburg; Charlottesville; Danville; and Bristol. Average per capita income was $19,671, nearly one thousand dollars more than the national average.

Lawrence Douglas Wilder, the first black man to be elected governor of a state, was inaugurated. Wilder, a Democrat from Richmond, served for four years, having held the job of lieutenant-governor for the previous four years.

1991

The General Assembly adopted square dancing as the official state folk dance, declaring that it "traces its ancestry to the English Country Dance and the French Ballroom Dance . . . and includes squares, rounds, clogging, contra, line, the Virginia Reel, and heritage dances." The Assembly also recognized the tiger swallowtail butterfly (*Papilio glaucus linne)* as the state insect.

1992

In early anticipation of the upcoming 2007 celebration of Virginia's four hundredth birthday, the Jamestown Archeological Assessment project was jointly initiated by the Colonial Williamsburg Foundation, the U. S. National Park Service, and the College of William and Mary. Its purpose is to reexamine and redefine Jamestown's past in light of new scientific and technological disciplines.

1993

The Bivalve Mollusk *(Chesapecten jeffersonius)* which was common in the Chesapeake Bay millions of years ago was named the Commonwealth's official state fossil. It was first discovered in 1687. Its Latin name, which was bestowed later, honors both the Bay and Thomas Jefferson, who had a great appreciation for natural history.

1994

George Felix Allen from Albemarle County was inaugurated governor of the Commonwealth. He was the first Republican to fill the office since 1982.

1995

By the end of this second full year of archaeological exploration at Jamestown, scientists led by Dr. Bill Kelso had retrieved some 800,000 artifacts from the site, many of them dating all the way back to the years surrounding the first settlement. Among the most exciting finds was the discovery of the footprint of the first fort, thereby refuting the age-old assumption that the palisade had been lost to the depths of the nearby James River.

1996

The U. S. Supreme Court ruled that the policy of all-male admission practiced by the Virginia Military Institute (VMI) was unconstitutional.

1997

The official Commonwealth song, *Carry Me Back to Old Virginia,* adopted in 1940, was retired.

The total value of goods and services produced by the Commonwealth exceeded 209 billion dollars.

1998

James Stuart Gilmore, III, a resident of Henrico County, and the Commonwealth's former attorney-general, became the governor of Virginia.

Moses Malone of Petersburg, the first American basketball player to join professional ranks directly out of high school, was named one of the National Basketball Association's top fifty players of all time.

Dwight Stephenson, a graduate of Hampton High School and considered by many to be the greatest center to ever play professional football, was inducted into the Pro Football Hall of Fame in Canton, Ohio.

1999

The median price for a home in the Richmond-Petersburg area jumped to $128,500.

2000

The Commonwealth's population reached more than 7,000,000, making it the twelfth largest state in the country.

The Blue Ridge Parkway, much of which traverses Virginia, led other properties in the National Park Service with nearly 20,000,000 visitors during the year. The George Washington Memorial Parkway came in sixth in visitations with almost 8,000,000.

2001

Virginia Tech beat Clemson 41 to 20 in the 2001 Gator Bowl played in Jacksonville, Florida.

On the morning of September 11, a giant jetliner commandeered by terrorists, crashed into the Pentagon in northern Virginia, killing 125 workers.

2002

Mark R. Warner, a telecommunications executive and former chairman of the Virginia Democratic Party, became governor of the Commonwealth.

2003

In September, Hurricane Isabel lashed the mid-Atlantic coastline bringing with it four billion dollars worth of property damage, much of it in Virginia. Fourteen people were killed in the Commonwealth. Almost two million others lost their electric power. Virginia was declared a federal disaster area, as were neighboring North Carolina and Maryland.

CBS Television News' first black correspondent, Hal Walker, died at his home in Reston at the age of seventy. Walker's twenty-seven-year career with CBS and ABC spanned the presidencies of Lyndon Johnson, Richard Nixon, Gerald Ford, Jimmy Carter, Ronald Reagan, George Bush, and Bill Clinton.

2004

President's Park, a historically-oriented facility dedicated to United States presidents – past, present, and future – opened in Williamsburg. The park features eighteen – to twenty-foot tall statues of all the men who have served as chief executive, along with other educational exhibits.

The Pentagon, located in northern Virginia across the Potomac River from Washington, D. C., was an engineering marvel when it was completed in 1943. The sheer logistics of operating the facility is mind-boggling as shown by this description from the Pentagon's official website.

The Pentagon, headquarters of the Department of Defense, is one of the world's largest office buildings. It is twice the size of the Merchandise Mart in Chicago, and has three times the floor space of the Empire State Building in New York. The National Capitol could fit into any one of the five wedge-shaped sections. There are very few people throughout the United States who do not have some knowledge of the Pentagon. Many have followed news stories emanating from the defense establishment housed in this building. However, relatively few people have had the opportunity to visit with us.
The Pentagon is virtually a city in itself. Approximately 23,000 employees, both military and civilian, contribute to the planning and execution of the defense of our country. These people arrive daily from Washington, D.C. and its suburbs over approximately 30 miles of access highways, including express bus lanes and one of the newest subway systems in our country. They ride past 200 acres of lawn to park approximately 8,770 cars in 16

parking lots; climb 131 stairways or ride 19 escalators to reach offices that occupy 3,705,793 square feet. While in the building, they tell time by 4,200 clocks, drink from 691 water fountains, utilize 284 rest rooms, consume 4,500 cups of coffee, 1,700 pints of milk and 6,800 soft drinks prepared or served by a restaurant staff of 230 persons and dispensed in 1 dining room, 2 cafeterias, 6 snack bars, and an outdoor snack bar. The restaurant service is a privately run civilian operation under contract to the Pentagon. Over 200,000 telephone calls are made daily through phones connected by 100,000 miles of telephone cable. The Defense Post Office handles about 1,200,000 pieces of mail monthly. Various libraries support our personnel in research and completion of their work. The Army Library alone provides 300,000 publications and 1,700 periodicals in various languages. Stripped of its occupants, furniture and various decorations, the building alone is an extraordinary structure. Built during the early years of World War II, it is still thought of as one of the most efficient office buildings in the world. Despite 17.5 miles of corridors it takes only seven minutes to walk between any two points in the building. The original site was nothing more than wasteland, swamps and dumps. 5.5 million cubic yards of earth, and 41,492 concrete piles contributed to the foundation of the building. Additionally, 680,000 tons of sand and gravel, dredged from the nearby Potomac River, were processed into 435,000 cubic yards of concrete and molded into the Pentagon form. The building was constructed in the remarkably short time of 16 months and completed on January 15, 1943 at an approximate cost of $83 million. It consolidated 17 buildings of the War Department and returned its investment within seven years.

Photograph courtesy of the National Archives.

Bibliography

Abbot, William W. *A Virginia Chronology 1585-1783*. Williamsburg: The Virginia 350th Anniversary Celebration Corporation, 1957.

Aikman, Lonnelle. *Rider With Destiny: George Washington*. McLean, Virginia: Link Press, 1983.

Alvord, Clarence Walworth and Lee Bidgood. *The First Explorations of the Trans-Allegheny Region by the Virginians 1650-1674*. Reprint. Baltimore: Clearfield Company Inc., 1996.

Ames, Susie M. *Reading, Writing, and Arithmetic in Virginia, 1607-1699*. Williamsburg: The Virginia 350th Anniversary Celebration Corporation, 1957.

Bemis, Samuel M., introduction. *The Three Charters of the Virginia Company of London*. Williamsburg: The Virginia 350th Anniversary Celebration Corporation, 1957.

Billings, Warren M. *Virginia's Viceroy, Their Majesties' Governor General: Francis Howard, Baron Howard of Effingham*. Fairfax, Virginia: George Mason University Press, 1991.

Bridenbaugh, Carl. *Jamestown 1544-1699.* New York: Oxford University Press, 1980.

Brydon, George MacLaren. *Religious Life Of Virginia In The Seventeenth Century.* Williamsburg: The Virginia 350th Anniversary Celebration Corporation, 1957.

Carrier, Lyman. *Agriculture in Virginia, 1607-1699.* Williamsburg: The Virginia 350th Anniversary Celebration Corporation, 1957.

Carruth, Gorton. *The Encyclopedia of American Facts & Dates.* 8th ed. New York: Harper & Row Publishers, 1987.

Cotter, John L. and J. Paul Hudson. *New Discoveries at Jamestown.* Washington, D. C.: Government Printing Office, 1957.

Craven, Wesley Frank. *The Virginia Company Of London, 1606-1624.* Williamsburg: The Virginia 350th Anniversary Celebration Corporation, 1957.

Current, Richard N. and T. Harry Williams, Frank Freidel, and Alan Brinkley. *American History: A Survey. Vol. I: To 1877.* 6th ed. New York: Alfred A. Knopf, 1983.

Crutchfield, James A. *America's Yesteryears.* Franklin, Tennessee: Cool Springs Press, 1996.

—————————————————. *Defining Moments in American History.* Williamsburg: Presidents Park, Inc., 2004.

—————————————————. *Mountain Men of the American West.* Boise, Idaho: Tamarack Books, 1997.

Delderfield, Eric R. and D. V. Cook. *Kings and Queens of England.* New York: Stein and Day, Inc. 1972.

Evans, Cerinda W. *Some Notes On Shipbuilding and Shipping In Colonial Virginia.* Williamsburg: The Virginia 350th Anniversary Celebration Corporation, 1957.

Fallows, Arthur. *Journal of Arthur Fallows.* Reprint. NP: Readex Microprint, 1966.

Faust, Patricia L., ed. *Historical Times Illustrated Encyclopedia of the Civil War.* New York: Harper & Row Publishers, 1986.

Forman, Henry Chandlee. *Virginia Architecture In The Seventeenth Century.* Williamsburg: The Virginia 350th Anniversary Celebration Corporation, 1957.

Fullinwider, Rowena and James A. Crutchfield and Winette Sparkman Jeffery. *Celebrate Virginia!* Nashville: Cool Springs Press, 2002.

Gabriel, Ralph H., editor. *The Pageant of America.* 15 vols. New Haven, Connecticut: Yale University Press, 1925-29.

Goodwin, Rutherfoord. *A Brief & True Report Concerning Williamsburg in Virginia.* 3rd ed. Williamsburg: The Colonial Williamsburg Foundation, 1977.

Hale, Nathaniel C. *Virginia Venturer: A Historical Biography of William Claiborne 1600-1677.* Richmond: The Dietz Press, 1951.

Harriot, Thomas. *A Briefe and True Report of the New Found Land of Virginia.* Frankfort, Germany, 1590. Facsimile, New York: Dover Publications, Inc., 1972.

Hatch, Jr., Charles E. *The First Seventeen Years: Virginia, 1607-1624.* Williamsburg: The Virginia 350th Anniversary Celebration Corporation, 1957.

Herndon, Melvin. *Tobacco In Colonial Virginia.* Williamsburg: The Virginia 350th Anniversary Celebration Corporation, 1957.

Hiden, Martha W. *How Justice Grew, Virginia Counties: An Abstract of Their Formation.* Williamsburg: The Virginia 350th Anniversary Celebration Corporation, 1957.

Hudson, J. Paul. *A Pictorial Booklet On Early Jamestown Commodities And Industries.* Williamsburg: The Virginia 350th Anniversary Celebration Corporation, 1957.

Hughes, Thomas P. *Medicine In Virginia, 1607-1699.* Williamsburg: The Virginia 350th Anniversary Celebration Corporation, 1957.

Hume, Ivor Noel. "First Look at a Lost Virginia Settlement." *National Geographic* Volume 155, No. 6, pp. 734-767. Washington, D. C.: The National Geographic Society, 1979.

——————————. *In Search of This & That: Tales From an Archaeologist's Quest.* Williamsburg: The Colonial Williamsburg Foundation, 1996.

——————————. *Martin's Hundred.* New York: Alfred A. Knopf, 1982.

——————————. "New Clues to Virginia's Lost Settlement." *National Geographic* Volume 161, No. 1, pp. 52-77. Washington, D. C.: The National Geographic Society, 1982.

——————————. *The Virginia Adventure: Roanoke to Jamestown.* New York: Alfred A. Knopf, 1998.

Jackson, Donald. *A Year at Monticello, 1795.* Golden, Colorado: Fulcrum, Inc., 1989.

Jester, Annie Lash. *Domestic Life in Virginia in the Seventeenth Century.* Williamsburg: The Virginia 350th Anniversary Celebration Corporation, 1957.

Kelso, William M. et al. *Rediscovering Jamestown: The Search for the 1607 James Fort.* 7 vols. Jamestown, Virginia: The Association for the Preservation of Virginia Antiquities, 1995-2001.

Kleinknecht, C. Fred. *Anchor of Liberty.* Washington, D. C.: The Supreme Council, Thirty-Third Degree Ancient and Accepted Scottish Rite of Freemasonry, 1987.

Lederer, John. *The Discoveries of John Lederer.* Reprint. Charlottsville: University of Virginia Press, 1958.

McCartney, Martha W. *Jamestown: An American Legacy.* NP: Eastern National, 2001.

McCary, Ben C. *Indians in Seventeenth-Century Virginia.* Williamsburg: The Virginia 350th Anniversary Celebration Corporation, 1957.

—————————————-. *John Smith's Map of Virginia With a Brief Account of its History.* Williamsburg: The Virginia 350th Anniversary Celebration Corporation, 1957.

McMurtrie, Douglas C. *The First Printing in Virginia.* Vienna, Austria: Herbert Reichner Verlag, 1935.

Morris, Richard B., ed. *Encyclopedia of American History.* 6th ed. New York: Harper & Row Publishers, 1982.

Morton, Richard L. *Struggle Against Tyranny, And The Beginning Of A New Era: Virginia, 1677-1699.* Williamsburg: The Virginia 350th Anniversary Celebration Corporation, 1957.

National Park Service. *Chesapeake and Ohio Canal.* Washington, D. C.: GPO, 1991.

———————————————. *Jamestown Archeological Assessment.* Washington, D. C.: GPO, ND.

Olmert, Michael and Suzanne E. Coffman. *Official Guide to Colonial Williamsburg.* New Edition. Williamsburg: The Colonial Williamsburg Foundation, 1998.

Randolph, Mary. *The Virginia House-Wife.* Reprint. Columbia, South Carolina: University of South Carolina Press, 1984.

Robinson, W. Stitt. *Mother Earth: Land Grants in Virginia, 1607-1699.* Williamsburg: The Virginia 350th Anniversary Celebration Corporation, 1957.

————————. *The Southern Colonial Frontier, 1607-1763.* Albuquerque: University of New Mexico Press, 1979.

Ross, George E. *Know Your Presidents and Their Wives.* Chicago: Rand McNally & Co., 1960.

Salmon, Emily J. and Edward D. C. Campbell, Jr., ed. *The Hornbook of Virginia History.* 4th ed. Richmond: The Library of Virginia, 1994.

Salmon, John S., compiler. *A Guidebook to Virginia's Historical Markers.* Revised and Expanded Edition. Charlottesville: University Press of Virginia, 1994.

Swem, E. G. and John M. Jennings. *A Selected Bibliography of Virginia, 1607-1699.* Williamsburg: The Virginia 350th Anniversary Celebration Corporation, 1957.

The Annals of America. Vols. 1 and 2. Chicago: Encyclopaedia Britannica Inc., 1968.

Trager, James. *The People's Chronology.* New York: Henry Holt & Company, 1994.

Tunis, Edwin. *Shaw's Fortune: The Picture Story of a Colonial Plantation.* Cleveland, Ohio: The World Publishing Company, 1966.

Virginia Historical Society. *Reluctant Ratifiers: Virginia Considers the Federal Constitution.* Richmond: Virginia Historical Society, 1988.

Washburn, Wilcomb E. *Virginia Under Charles I And Cromwell, 1625-1660.* Williamsburg: The Virginia 350th Anniversary Celebration Corporation, 1957.

Werstein, Irving. *1776: The Adventure of the American Revolution Told in Pictures.* New York: Cooper Square Publishers Inc. 1976.

Wertenbaker, Thomas J. *Bacon's Rebellion, 1676.* Williamsburg: The Virginia 350th Anniversary Celebration Corporation, 1957.

————————————. *The Government of Virginia In The Seventeenth Century.* Williamsburg: The Virginia 350th Anniversary Celebration Corporation, 1957.

Wharton, James. *The Bounty Of The Chesapeake.* Williamsburg: The Virginia 350th Anniversary Celebration Corporation, 1957.

Whitney, David C. *Colonial Spirit of '76: The People of the Revolution.* Chicago: Encyclopaedia Britannica Educational Corporation, 1974.

Wilson, Jr., Vincent. *The Book of the Founding Fathers.* Brookeville, Maryland: American History Research Associates, 1974.

Zwelling, Shomer S. *Quest for a Cure: The Public Hospital in Williamsburg, Virginia, 1773-1885.* Williamsburg: The Colonial Williamsburg Foundation, 1985.

Index

A

A Map of Virginia, With a Description of the Country, the Commodities, People, Government and Religion 9

A Perfect Description of Virginia 21

A Supplement to the Negro's & Indians Advocate: or, Some Further Considerations and Proposals for the Effectual and Speedy Carrying of the Negro's Christianity in our Plantations 31

A Treatise on Gardening 68

A True Discourse of the Present Estate of Virginia 10

Abby Aldrich Rockefeller Folk Art Museum 120

Abington 114

Accomac County 16,19

Accomack 56

Accomack County 25,26

Act of Union 36

Adams, John 44,69,70,76,79

Adams, John Quincy 76,78,79

Adney Gap 27

African slaves 12

African-Americans 27

Afton Mountain 114

Agricultural Extension Service 107

Alabama 75,101

Albany, New York 46

Albemarle County 45,46,50,54,57, 60,128

Alexandria 42,47,48,51,52,82,90, 114,115

Alexandria County 84

Alexandria's Christ Church 57

Allan, Edgar Poe 73

Alleghany County 77,115

Allegheny Mountains 27

Allen, George Felix 128

Amadas, Philip 2

Ambler, Richard 57

Amelia County 44,50,66,116

America 2,4,9

America Eats 116

American Dogwood 109

American Foxhound 122

Lee, Henry "Lighthorse Harry"
52,72,115
Lee, Richard Henry 44,57
Lee, Robert E. 48,72,84,87,89,91,92,
96,99,102,103,115
Lee, Thomas 46
Lee's Army of Northern Virginia 93
Letcher, John 90
Levingston, William 40
Lewis and Clark 74
Lewis and Clark Expedition 57,71,75
Lewis, John L. 115
Lewis, Meriwether 56,57,71,72,82
Lexington 48,81,99,118
Lexington, Massachusetts 59
Liberia 79
Lincoln, Abraham 89,96,97
Lincoln, Benjamin 63
Liny, Robert 30
Little Falls of the Potomac River 79
London 3,10,14,15,22,28,31,36,
40,42,44
Lonesome Road Blues 113
Long Island of the Holston River 58
Loomis, Dr. Mahlon 97
Lord De La Warr 8
"Lord Dunmore's War" 58
Lords of Trade 41
Loudoun County 53
Louisa County 45,55
Louisiana 54,71
Louisiana Territory 72
Louisville, Kentucky 75
Lower Norfolk County 17,32
Loyal Company 46,47,50
Ludwell, Philip 31
Ludwell-Paradise House 112
Lunenburg County 46,50,55
Lynch, John 86
Lynchburg 86,102,104,106,109,
112,114,127
Lyndhurst Methodist Church 120

M

MacArthur, Douglas 118
MacKaye, Benton 112
Maddison, Isaac 15
Madison County 67,76
Madison, James 50,59,66,68,72,74,76
Magazine at Williamsburg 59
Maine 4
Malone, Dumas 124,125
Malone, Moses 128
Mandan Indians 71
Manufacturing Society of
Williamsburg 61
Marion County 90
Marquis de Lafayette 77
Marshall, George C. 117,118,119
Marshall, George Catlett 104
Marshall, James William 99
Marshall, John 51,70,81,122
Marshall Plan 117
Martin, John 15
Martin, Joseph 113
Martin's Hundred 14,122
Martinsville 113
Mary II 32
Maryland 16,28,34,43,51,66,92
Mason, George 28,42,46,67
Massachusetts 76,79
Mathews County 25,67
Mathews, Samuel 15
Mathews, Samuel, Jr. 24,25
Maury, Matthew Fontaine 72,82,84,85
Maybelle 113
Maynard, Lieutenant 40
Mayo, William 45
McClellan, George B. 91,92
McComb, John, Jr. 67
McCormack, Cyrus 80,83
McKinley, William 119
McLean House 96
Meade, George G. 93
Meadow Farm 126
Mecklenburg County 37,55

S